Les PETITS MACARONS

Colorful French Confections to Make at Home

Kathryn Gordon & Anne E. McBride

RUNNING PRESS
PHILADELPHIA · LONDON

© 2011 by Kathryn Gordon and Anne E. McBride
Photographs © 2011 by Steve Legato
Published by Running Press,
A Member of the Perseus Books Group

All rights reserved under the Pan-American and International Copyright Conventions
Printed in China

Books published by Running Press are available at special discounts for bulk purchases in the United States by corporations, institutions, and other organizations. For more information, please contact the Special Markets Department at the Perseus Books Group, 2300 Chestnut Street, Suite 200, Philadelphia, PA 19103, or call (800) 810-4145, ext. 5000, or e-mail special.markets@perseusbooks.com.

ISBN 978-0-7624-4258-4
Library of Congress Control Number: 2010941544

E-book ISBN 978-0-7624-4363-5

9   8   7
Digit on the right indicates the number of this printing

Cover and interior design by Amanda Richmond
Edited by Kristen Green Wiewora
Typography: Neutra and Mrs. Eaves

The publisher would like to thank: Crate & Barrel, King of Prussia, PA; Manor Home & Gifts, Philadelphia, PA; Scarlett Alley, Philadelphia, PA; and Sur la Table, King of Prussia, PA; for graciously loaning merchandise to be used in the photography.

Running Press Book Publishers
2300 Chestnut Street
Philadelphia, PA 19103-4371

Visit us on the web!
www.runningpresscooks.com

to JESSIE RILEY & RON McBRIDE,

who indulge our macaron obsession

CONTENTS

ALL ABOUT MACARONS 7 ★ *A Brief History 10* ★

Skin and Feet 14 ★ *The Four Main Ingredients 16* ★

BEFORE YOU BAKE 24 ★ **BASE MACARON RECIPES 34** ★

French Meringue Method 40 ★ *Italian Meringue Method 44* ★

Swiss Meringue Method 51 ★ *Kathryn's Easiest French Macaron Method 55*

★ **SWEET SHELLS 64** ★ **SAVORY SHELLS 94** ★ **GANACHE**

FILLINGS 104 ★ **CREAMY FILLINGS 128**

★ **CARAMEL FILLINGS 158** ★ **FROZEN FILLINGS 174**

★ **FRUIT-BASED FILLINGS 184** ★ **FAVORITE AMERICAN**

CLASSICS 204 ★ **SAVORY FILLINGS 218**

★ **FOR LESS-THAN-PERFECT MACARONS 238**

★ **TROUBLESHOOTING GUIDE 249** ★ **RESOURCES 257** ★

ACKNOWLEDGMENTS 261 ★ **INDEX 264**

ALL ABOUT MACARONS

Macarons first capture our attention with tantalizing colors—light green, golden yellow, hot pink, or velvety brown—that give them the appearance of jewels in a pastry shop case. But they do not stand on looks alone. The contrast between their crisp shells and soft fillings make them the most perfect way to satisfy a craving. Evoking timeless images of polished Parisians nibbling in delicate tea salons or sophisticated *pâtisseries*, they transport us to a more elegant time and place in just two bites.

I first began making macarons more than fifteen years ago, when I was working at The Rainbow Room in New York City. We served them as mignardises to diners who would momentarily turn away from the stunning views to admire them—a pleasure more instantaneous, more within reach. Ever since that time I've been fascinated with macarons, experimenting with different shell and filling flavors and always looking for them when traveling. I am fortunate to go to France every year, so my research is always fresh—and delicious. Not all macarons are created equal. Some are light and airy, others almost cake-like. Some have almost no shell and are very delicate, and others have a very thick shell that resists the bite.

In 2003, this interest led me to teach just one class on the subject at the

Institute of Culinary Education in New York, where I had just begun working. Macarons have become so popular that I now offer a series of those classes, covering anything from savory to holiday macarons. I have also begun leading a macaron walking tour, for which I take students to various New York pastry shops. More recently, I have noticed more people asking about macarons because they are gluten-free, providing those suffering from celiac disease or gluten sensitivity with a treat they can consume without consequences.

The macaron should be one of the easiest cookies to make; after all, it only includes four ingredients. It speaks to its complexity, then, and makes it even more special, that top-ranked pastry chefs around the world can't agree on how to combine these ingredients to turn them into the footed, smooth-shelled marvel we love. Different macaron production techniques have evolved, primarily related to the meringue component. But my theory is simply that chefs learned to make a macaron where they first trained—as I did. Under the "if it's not broke, don't fix it" theory, unless they encounter a persistent issue, I think that most chefs have not thought much about what really makes their favorite macaron method work, and simply believe their method to be the best one. The one technique they will probably agree on is the prolonged folding required to incorporate all the ingredients, called *macaronner* (more on this unusual technique in a moment).

About twelve years ago, I was privileged to become involved in the World Pastry Forum, an annual gathering of professional chefs. This unparalleled access allowed me to interview every world-champion pastry chef I met about his or her method, to figure out what truly works and what can be fixed at various stages of the process. This book is a result of those discussions. It includes three different base methods for meringues, along with all the tips, tricks, and troubleshooting techniques I've ever come across. But one word of caution: Although experienced bakers do occasionally switch their production method (going from a French meringue to an Italian meringue base, for example), I believe strongly that there is no single holy grail. When you find the meringue procedure—and whatever additional tricks you might need—that works for you, stay with that base method. You may have a "bad macaron day," as even the best pâtissiers confess to having. But the best approach is to practice that technique, keep a diary of what you did, and evolve flavor variations off that base.

MACARON OR MACAROONS?

THE FRENCH-STYLE COOKIE (WHAT WE CALL THE PARISIAN MACARON, but in France refers to all sorts of macarons) is spelled with only one "o," and pronounced mah-kah-rohn. The final syllable is a very nasal sound that doesn't quite exist in English, almost as if saying "round" but with lips tightly pursed, and the "nd" is silent. No syllable is emphasized. The American macaroon, pronounced mah-kah-ROON, refers most often to unleavened cookies made with sweetened coconut flakes or with almond paste.

A Brief History

The lore of macarons often suggests that Catherine de' Medici brought them to France in 1533 when she married Henry II. Many similar stories of imported foods and techniques revolve around her and her Italian chefs, not all of them true, so accurate or not, we'll accept that this is part of the macaron's myth.

The word macaron comes from the Italian *maccherone* or *macaroni*, which a 1650 volume, *Les Origines de la Langue Françoise*, defines as "a pasta dish with cheese." Macaron long referred not just to a cookie, but a savory preparation as well, which seems to have consisted of lumps of flour-based "paste" cooked with spices and grated cheese and served with a liquid. The Italian term itself is of Greek origin, from the word for kneading or mixing, from which "cook" and "baker" are then derived. *Maccare*, an Italian verb that signifies "to beat" or "to pound," is another related meaning. A 1673 French-English dictionary defines macaron as "little Fritter-like Buns, or thick Losenges, compounded of Sugar, Almonds, Rosewater, and Musk, pounded together, and baked with gentle fire."

Almond-based foodstuffs were popular in the Middle Ages already. Macarons are often thought to have appeared in the eighth century in Venetian monasteries (after almonds arrived in Italy with the Arabs), with some sources also mentioning a French abbey in Cormery that supposedly began making them in 791, even though some believe that this particular macaron emerged only in the nineteenth century.

One way or another, a cookie made from almonds and sugar became popular in France, where various cities, such as Paris, Reims, Montmorillon, Saint-Jean-de-Luz, and Amiens, went on to develop it into their own specialties. Nuns were often the driving force behind macarons, which they made for both nutritional and commercial purposes (baked goods, honey, and other such food products were a source of revenue for most monastic orders, which had very limited ways of making money). Such is the case in Nancy, another French city famous for its macarons, which are flatter than Parisian macarons and don't have a smooth surface. In the late eighteenth century, the nuns of Les Dames du Saint Sacrement's Convent, who were forbidden from eating meat, started making macarons because they were nutritious. After the closing of the convent at the French Revolution, two of the sisters began selling the macarons in order to make a living. They became legendary as "les Soeurs Macarons," (the Macaron Sisters) to the point that a street now bears that name in Nancy.

By the middle of the seventeenth century, recipes for macarons had begun appearing in French cookbooks. François Pierre de La Varenne's *Le Pâtissier François,* published in 1653, mentions macarons several times as elements of other recipes, seemingly to give them body (they continue to appear through the nineteenth century at least). The 1692 *Nouvelle Instruction pour les Confitures, les Liqueurs, et les Fruits* states that macarons are a combination of sweet almonds, sugar, and egg white, and offers instructions that include flavoring the batter with orange blossom water and icing them once baked, if desired. From that point on, macarons appear regularly in cookbooks. And if nineteenth century books about Paris are to be believed, by then the city was teeming with macaron street vendors.

The macaron as we now best know it—two shells sandwiching a filling—is a more recent invention. Ladurée, the famed Parisian tea salon and pastry shop perhaps most associated with them today, was founded in 1862, but it was not until the early twentieth century that Pierre Desfontaines, second cousin of Louis Ernest Ladurée, had the idea of piping ganache on a shell and topping it with another. It is now the ubiquitous way to sell and serve Parisian-style macarons—called *gerbet*, a name that still appears today—around the globe, and perhaps only the blue box of Tiffany's rivals Ladurée's elegant green box in the gasp it might inspire.

WHAT SHOULD A PARISIAN MACARON LOOK AND TASTE LIKE?

SINCE MACARONS ARE SO SPECIALIZED, PEOPLE ARE NOT ALWAYS sure of what to expect when eating a macaron, let alone when baking one. They might never have eaten one before and have no point of reference. Look for three things:

* **A SLIGHTLY SHINY, THIN SHELL WITH A SLIGHT CRUNCH** that resists the teeth for a second when you bite into it; it should not be so delicate that it melts into the filling, or so thick that it is mostly crust;

* **A PROPORTIONAL, NARROW FOOT AROUND THE SHELL** of the macaron, certainly not non-existent; and

* **AN INTERIOR THAT IS SOFT, MOIST, AND ONLY SLIGHTLY CHEWY** (excessive chewiness can be a sign of excessive baking time); the shell and filling, eaten together, should not be excessively sweet.

13

ALL ABOUT MACARONS

Skin and Feet

es, macarons have been very much anthropomorphized—that's how much we chefs care about them. The crust of the macaron shell is often called its "skin" in the pre- or early baking stages. When you very gently touch the piped shell after it has dried for a while (in or out of the oven), you can feel a barrier with your finger. It will feel a little dry, like a crust only about a hair's width thick. As the meringue expands in the oven, it pushes outward and upward. This expansion results in the formation of a foot: a round, even circle at the bottom of the shell that has more texture and is about two millimeters thick. Feet will not form in an oven that is too hot, where the macaron bakes too quickly and the crust itself cannot form properly. In such a case, the interior batter will still be moist, causing steam and therefore some bubbling; cracking is a typical result.

Some recipes advocate leaving the piped shells out for a few hours before baking, which lets them form a skin that then helps create crispy shells and proper feet. But macarons, like all meringues, are very sensitive to humidity: sugar attracts the moisture that is in the air. Other chefs believe that by letting the macarons form a skin at room temperature, moisture from the air may land on the shell, and instead might cause cracks to form. That's the theory I subscribe to. Christian Godineau, a pastry chef and owner of La Duchesse Anne in Saumur, France, taught me to put them in a very low temperature oven immediately after piping, to allow the skin to form in a dry environment. Then, when the skin has formed, I increase the heat to a typical temperature and the macaron shells begin baking.

THE ANATOMY OF A MACARON

SKIN:
The hair's width-thick crust of the macaron,
which forms as the piped shell dries in the oven.

FOOT:
A textured ring around the base of the shell, which forms
as moisture in the macaron turns to steam and rises.

The Four Main Ingredients

As we've established, macarons might have few ingredients, but each one carries much importance in the complete baking process. Here are some thoughts on each of the four main players, as well as on the supporting cast that contributes to making perfect—or nearly perfect—macarons.

Almond Flour

Almond flour, or almond meal, is simply almonds that are ground into an extremely fine powder. The almonds are usually blanched (de-skinned) before grinding, but not always. The whiter your almond flour, the whiter your final macarons, but unblanched almond flour will result in macarons that are just as tasty. Commercially milled flour is usually finer than home-ground almonds, but never as fine as wheat flour. It should be very dry and powdery when you rub some in your fingers. If one brand isn't working for you, or seems oily, try a different brand (see Resources, page 257, for mail-order options if the ones you find locally are not yielding good results). It can go rancid, so I divide it and store it in freezer-safe resealable plastic bags in the freezer. Commercially ground pistachio and hazelnut flours are also available.

DRYING ALMOND FLOUR

SLIGHTLY WET OR OILY ALMOND FLOUR CAN CAUSE CRACKED MAC-
aron shells. If you store your flour in the refrigerator or freezer, drying it before
using—to remove any moisture from storage—will improve the structure and shape of
your macarons and reduce the risk of cracks.

Preheat the oven to 200°F (95°C).

Spread the almond flour on a baking sheet and bake it for 30 minutes. Remove the
flour from the oven and let it cool completely before proceeding with the recipe.

Confectioners' Sugar

Confectioners' sugar is one of the key elements of macarons. Its fine structure
means that it is completely incorporated into the ground nuts, creating what
is called *tant-pour-tant* in pastry: an equal percentage of almond flour and confectioners' sugar that is at the base of many cookies. It contributes to the macaron's smooth texture by dissolving quickly into egg whites.

American confectioners' sugar contains cornstarch to keep it from clump-
ing. Certain French chefs import their own starch-free confectioners' sugar
from France in order to make macarons here, but regular supermarket confectioners' sugar (used in all the recipes in this book) works just fine. Wrap any
leftover confectioners' sugar tightly so that it does not clump up until your
next baking session, and store it at room temperature.

Granulated Sugar

Granulated sugar is the pure white form of sugar that is used to build the meringue structure of the macaron in combination with egg whites. Some chefs prefer to use superfine sugar instead, believing that the finer crystal size helps form a stable meringue more quickly when combining with the water and protein from the egg whites. The recipes here use regular granulated sugar, but if you feel like experimenting, try using superfine sugar in French or Swiss meringues (it won't matter much for Italian meringue because the sugar is cooked into a fully dissolved syrup).

Egg Whites

Egg whites provide the proteins necessary to the structure of macarons. Water constitutes 90 percent of the egg white, and protein makes up the rest. When air is beaten into it, it foams up. As Harold McGee explains it in *On Food and Cooking*, the white's proteins "unfold and bond to each other." Aged egg whites, in which some of the water has evaporated and proteins have thinned, foam more quickly and generally produce smoother, more even macarons. See the Note on Egg Whites (opposite) for details on aging your eggs before baking.

When whisking egg whites, a medium speed will result in more stability than a meringue whipped quickly strictly on high speed. However, I always turn the mixer speed up to high at the very end of the process for about three seconds, to obtain the maximum volume before incorporating the dry ingredients.

NOTE ON EGG WHITES

"AGED" EGG WHITES HAVE A CONCENTRATED PROTEIN STRUCTURE that works best when forming the meringue that is the macarons' whole infrastructure. Fresh eggs make for a less solid shell structure that can cause macarons to crack or not take shape properly. You can safely age egg whites in the refrigerator for several days, especially since they are then baked. Even if you don't have time to do so (sometimes you just must make macarons right now), letting them sit a few hours on your kitchen counter before baking will help, as will the addition of powdered egg white (see page 20).

Two to five days before baking macarons, separate four egg whites. Place them in a container, whisk them until they are thoroughly combined, and cover the top of the container with plastic wrap. Pole holes in the plastic wrap so that air can reach the whites and evaporate of some of their water content, and leave them refrigerated until ready to bake. Remove them from the refrigerator two hours before baking, so that they reach room temperature and can whip to a high volume. Measure the exact amount of egg white needed before using, whisking them again if needed.

Supporting Ingredients

POWDERED EGG WHITE: Powdered egg white is a pasteurized product created by freeze-drying egg whites to extract their water. You will find it in the baking aisle of most supermarkets (Just Whites is a popular brand) or online. I use it when making French meringue-based macarons, which tend to spread a bit more than Swiss or Italian, but also add a small quantity (from just a pinch up to about ¼ teaspoon per egg white) if the weather is very humid, regardless of the method used. If you are located in a very dry climate, you won't need powdered egg white for anything but Kathryn's Easiest French Macaron Method.

Adding dehydrated powdered egg white to fresh egg whites strengthens the protein bonds that form when beating them, since proportionately, there is less water per egg. You can also use it if you haven't had a chance to age your eggs for several days: add ½ teaspoon of egg white powder per egg white that you need in the recipe, whisking it into the "real" egg whites before proceeding.

CREAM OF TARTAR: Adding acid, such as cream of tartar or lemon juice, at the beginning of the egg whipping process helps stabilize the egg white foam and prevents overwhipping the meringue. The acid can be particularly helpful if you are making meringue with freshly separated egg whites (unaged). You can whip a glossy, non-grainy meringue without cream of tartar in most situations, but if you have it, use it: the resulting meringue will be firmer and more stable.

SALT: Salt acts as a flavor balancer and enhancer in nut-based recipes. I add it in with the recipe's other dry ingredients so it does not affect the foaming power of the egg whites. I prefer fine sea salt for all baking, which easily dissolves in batters, and use salt from France because I have found it to be the most flavorful. Baleine, a fine sea salt formed by natural evaporation, is available in most grocery stores and sold in cylindrical blue canisters.

When flavor and texture both matter, such as with salted caramel fillings, you need to use fleur de sel—"flower of the sea." This salt is hand-raked off shallow clay beds near Brittany, a process that raises its price tag; it is a finishing salt, meant to be added to a savory dish once it is cooked. When used in caramels and ganaches, it is often stirred in, but can also be sprinkled on top of a filling or a shell; its strong flavor and crunchy texture providing maximum impact.

FOOD COLORING: A major appeal of macarons is their colorful appearance, which typically indicates their flavor. A pink macaron will taste like strawberry or raspberry, a yellow one like mango, a green one like pistachio, and a dark brown one like chocolate. Colorings exist in liquid, gel, paste, or powder form (see Resources, page 257). You will find liquid coloring in the baking aisle of most supermarkets, but usually only in basic colors. When we specify a type of color, such as mint green, we refer to the colorings found in specialty baking stores, which carry a wide range of types and shades of food colorings. You can use basic colorings instead; the shells' colors will just not be as subtle and your range of possible colors might be more limited. I prefer gels to liquids, but either will work so use what you like best or have on hand. Traditional light pastel colors can be achieved with just a few drops of liquid or gel, but the deepest colors, particularly jewel-tone shades or dark solids, such as black, require powders. It would take too much liquid coloring to achieve those results, which would destabilize the structure of the meringue.

Add in the liquid, gel, or paste coloring towards the end of the macaronnage stage (page 26), when the batter appears to be about two-thirds mixed. If you add the food color too early, the air you are whisking into the batter will lighten the color (for example, red may turn pink). It will also keep you from overfolding the batter. Pulse powdered colors in the food processor together with the confectioners' sugar and almond flour at the beginning of the process.

FLAVOR COMPOUNDS: Concentrated flavor compounds allow you to flavor macaron shells without changing the composition of the ingredients and adding too much liquid to the base. Think of them as "super gels,"

with a ketchup-like consistency. They are sold in jars and exist in a wide range of flavors, such as passion fruit, violet, and licorice. These compounds are typically sold wholesale, but a number of retailers are now offering quantities small enough for home bakers. See Resources, page 257, for addresses. To use them, fold 3 tablespoons (60 grams) of the compound into the macaron base (any method will do) just before it reaches the macaronnage stage.

Before You Bake

Read this section carefully before baking your first batch of macarons, and continue to revisit it as you get more and more familiar with the techniques and recipes. The more knowledge and practice you have, the higher your rate of success.

For Macaron Shells

MEASURING INGREDIENTS: Everyone measures dry ingredients differently, which is why using weight measurements ensures the most precision in baking. The recipes in this book give you both options: to use a scale (digital scales can be found in most kitchenware and department stores for about $30) or measuring cups and spoons.

Dry ingredients, such as flour, are often ingredients in which wide variations in measurements appear, since it depends on how much you pack into the measuring cup, how aerated the flour is, or if you scoop it into the cup or dip the cup into the flour bag, for example. The same is true of confectioners' sugar.

IN ALL THE RECIPES IN THIS BOOK, nut flours and confectioners' sugar were measured by firmly packing the ingredient into a measuring cup, as you would brown sugar. The eggs used are large.

PARCHMENT PAPER VS. SILICONE MATS: You can use parchment paper and obtain great macarons. I prefer using silicone baking mats (available for about $20 alongside baking equipment in most department and kitchenware stores; Silpat is a popular brand), which disperse the heat of the oven more evenly on the baking sheet and shield the bottom of the macarons better, since they are thicker than parchment paper. These mats should not be cut or stored folded, and are dishwasher safe. If possible, purchase at least two; this will allow you to immediately pipe a new batch of macarons while the ones just out of the oven cool on the mat.

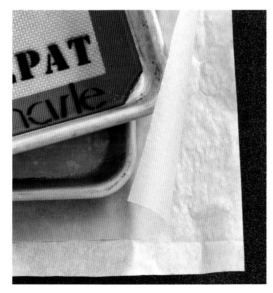

Parchment paper will flap around in a convection oven and ruin the smooth shells of the macarons. If you are baking in a convection oven, pipe a dab of batter under each of the four corners of the parchment paper; this will hold it in place. There is no need to do that with silicone baking mats, which are heavier.

IN RECIPES THAT USE AN ELECTRIC MIXER—including the base recipes—"medium" speed means medium on the high side, not low side, of mixer speeds. Speed levels vary from machine to machine, but this will be between 4 and 6.

WHIPPING EGG WHITES: When whipping a small amount of egg whites in a stand mixer, the whisk attachment might not make contact right away with the whites if the bowl is too big. To remedy that, lift the bowl slightly with your hands and hold it in place as the whisk turns for a minute or so, until the process looks to be underway.

MACARONNER (FOLDING THE INGREDIENTS TOGETHER): Folding the dry ingredients into the meringue is the key to obtaining the right structure for macarons. Not incorporating them enough might result in a meringue that is too strong to allow the formation of the feet and popped-up crust that characterize macarons, while folding them too much will cause the shells to crack or spread unevenly. You probably already know how to incorporate non-homogenous ingredients together through folding if you have made a cake or a mousse; this is often referred to as "J folding" (see box). Unlike most cake batters, which instruct you to fold "until just incorporated," here you will need to fold the ingredients until the batter is loose enough to drip down from the spatula back to the bowl in one continuous lava-like flow, which takes slightly longer than you might expect. This special step is called macaronner (also referred to here as the macaronnage stage or process).

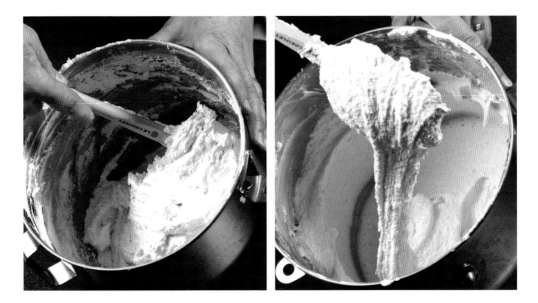

During the macaronnage process, you need to look for the beginning of movement in the batter; it will become slack, or loose, and just slightly shiny. To test that the viscosity is correct, once the ingredients appear to be just combined, use the spatula to lift some of the mixture about 3 inches above the bowl. If it retains a three-dimensional shape, fold it briefly again. Test repeatedly every time you stir, to make sure that you are not overmixing. When folded just enough, the mixture should fall right back into the bowl, with no stiffness, in one continuous drip. Folding by hand, it should take about 18 folds to complete this process. To double-check that the batter's viscosity is correct, slam the mixer bowl firmly on the counter: the batter should move and not hold a three-dimensional shape.

"J" FOLDING IS THE TERM USED WHEN COMBINING TWO OR MORE non-homogenous ingredients together, quickly and efficiently, by drawing a spatula through the middle of a batter as if forming the letter "J." See photos of the step-by-step technique below.

1. Bring the spatula down the middle of the batter.

2. Scrape it up toward the left-side quarter of the bowl (9 o'clock), forming the letter "J."

3. Rotate the bowl by 90 degrees and repeat the steps above.

4. Continue rotating the bowl and folding, so that in four folds you will have incorporated the ingredients in all four quadrants of the bowl.

PIPING TIPS: Piping macarons of different sizes onto the same baking sheet will yield poor results, because little ones will be hard and dry before the large ones are fully cooked. Even experienced production bakers often use a piping guide under the parchment paper or silicone baking mat to ensure even piping. We've made a downloadable guide available on our website, www.lespetits macarons.com. You can also make your own: Draw one circle of the size desired, and then use it as a stencil to draw circles on a sheet of paper the size of your baking sheet, drawing the circles about 1½ inches apart (to allow for spreading) across and down. Photocopy your guide so that you always have one handy.

A proper pastry bag will be the easiest tool to use to pipe. You can buy disposable ones in the baking aisle of most supermarkets, in specialty baking stores, and in the cake decorating aisle of craft stores. Resealable plastic bags are harder to handle, but will still work better than spoons. You can use two teaspoons or a ½-inch scoop if you are really averse to piping; the shells might not be as smooth, however.

When making mini, ½-inch macarons, cut a small, ¼-inch hole straight across the tip of the pastry piping bag. For small (1 inch or 3 centimeters) or large (2 inches or 6 centimeters) macarons, you will get the most consistent piping results with a ½-inch-wide piping tip. After a bit of practice, you will also obtain great results without the tip, by simply cutting a ½-inch opening straight across the bag (a precise, straight cut is key).

To refill the pastry bag with more batter

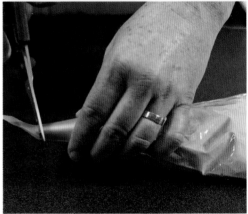

cleanly and easily, open the bag up and put it in a measuring cup to hold it in place. This will free up both your hands for refilling.

If you have more batter than will fit in your oven to bake at one time or to leave in your pastry bag, cover it so that it does not dry out and form a skin. Place a small piece of plastic wrap or waxed paper directly on the batter until you can pipe it.

BAKING TIPS: Professional kitchens abound with baking sheets, but that's not always the case with home kitchens. We've obtained the most consistent results when baking macaron shells on two baking sheets. If your oven bakes unevenly and your macarons consistently slope to one side, for example, invest in a third baking sheet, since it will resolve that problem by properly dispersing the heat that causes it. Rotating the baking sheets front to back as you increase the oven temperature after 15 minutes and rotate them again halfway through the second baking period, and even from the top to the bottom rack and vice versa in extreme cases, also helps.

If you have enough baking sheets to bake two batches of macarons at once, you may need to rotate them from top to bottom as well as front to back, if the top batch turns darker than the bottom one.

COOLING AND REMOVAL: Macaron shells are very delicate and subject to overheating, so after removing the baking sheets from the oven, immediately slide the silicone mat or parchment paper onto a cooling rack, your kitchen

counter, or wherever you can! Careful steaming can be helpful to loosen the shells. Lift the edge of the silicone mat or parchment carefully with a dry towel, and immediately pour 1 to 2 tablespoons of water under the mat or paper. Shake the baking sheet quickly, to create steam under the whole surface; this will help detach the macarons.

Let the macarons cool completely before attempting to remove them, because they are inclined to crack when warm. If you are lucky, they lift up without problems. If they stick slightly, you may need a metal off-set spatula to help slide them off by placing the spatula under the macaron and applying downward pressure, without pushing up into the shell. If the macarons appear very dry or are hard to remove from the parchment paper, place them in the freezer for two hours or leave them out at room temperature for up to one day before filling them.

FILLING TIPS: If you like more filling in your macaron, or are piping fillings that are a little looser in texture and need to be secured, carefully make an indentation in the underside of the shell by pushing it in with your thumb. You can then pipe or spoon the filling in this space, giving it more real estate in the shell.

Spread thicker, slightly chunky fillings on the shells with a spoon or a butter knife. Smooth fillings can be piped: Spoon it into a pastry bag, only filling it halfway, and cut a ½-inch opening at the tip (or use a ½-inch-wide piping tip). Pipe the filling on half of the shells, then top with another shell, and twist the sandwiched macaron slightly to secure the filling.

Most of the fillings in this book make 1 pint. Those with smaller yields are rich enough that a smaller amount suffices to fill the macarons; are paired with another filling; or need to be piped or spooned in smaller amounts, otherwise the sandwiched shells would slide apart.

REFRIGERATING TIPS: Keep macarons, filled or unfilled, in an airtight container in the refrigerator for up to three days. You can also wrap them tightly in plastic wrap. Bring them to room temperature before eating them, leaving them wrapped or boxed as they warm up to release any moisture that may have collected on the shells.

FREEZING TIP: Macarons filled with ganache, buttercream, or ice cream freeze very well—and taste delicious that way. They might even become a dangerous addiction, particularly since the freezer will keep them available at all times. Wrap them with plastic wrap in groups of six and put them in a container so that they don't get crushed. Store them in the freezer for up to one month. When removing them from the freezer, let them thaw out in the container, still wrapped. Moisture that is released as they warm up will cling to the plastic wrap rather than to the macarons, and they will remain crispy. Don't freeze macarons filled with pastry cream or fruit-based fillings, which will become too soggy when thawing out.

BASE MACARON RECIPES

Parisian-style macarons are traditionally meringue-based, which means that they contain egg whites and sugar combined in an airy mixture that will rise and then crisp upon baking. Three different methods exist for meringues: Italian, French, and Swiss. Their variations depend on how the sugar is added to the egg whites and whether or not the sugar is heated. Most cookbooks offer just one recipe for macarons, because each chef has his or her favorite and tends to advocate for that one only. Although we have our favorite, too, here we offer recipes for each of the meringue methods, so that you can test them and determine not only which one you prefer, but which one works best for your skills and your equipment.

A key difference among the methods resides in the way in which the ideal protein structure of the meringue is achieved. For a Swiss meringue, the egg whites are cooked with the sugar; in an Italian meringue, the cooked sugar syrup is poured into the egg whites as they are being whipped; and in a French meringue, the egg whites and sugar are beaten together cold. Many production bakers prefer Italian meringue because it is the most consistently reliable. The Swiss meringue will be particularly useful if you have trouble with either method because of a less-than-reliable oven, since it combines the advantages of the other two methods (but makes for a stiffer meringue that can be harder to pipe). Other than Kathryn's Easiest French Macaron Method (page 35), French meringue is the simplest one, since it requires minimal equipment and no manipulation of hot sugar.

The degree to which the egg whites are pre-cooked—or not—varies within these methods. That's not critical, because the macarons will all fully bake in the oven, regardless of how they start out. For all meringue methods, however, the most important point is to get the meringue "right." It shouldn't be overwhipped (which could result in cracked shells), or break down, which will make it difficult to incorporate the dry ingredients, resulting in low yield and/or spreading issues. It is important to obtain the glossy, smooth, good-bodied meringue with a firm peak that forms the infrastructure of the macaron.

You will find the base recipes to be extremely detailed. It does not mean that making macarons is beyond the reach of anyone but the most accomplished pastry chef—on the contrary—but rather, we want to share with you all the tricks learned through more than fifteen years of making macarons.

THE FIRST TIME YOU MAKE MACARONS AT HOME, pipe and bake just a couple once your batter is ready. This will allow you to troubleshoot any oven or batter issues before baking the full batch. If they do not bake perfectly, consult the Troubleshooting Guide, page 249.

Preparation

EQUIPMENT

2 baking sheets

Silicone mats or parchment paper

Food processor

Fine-mesh strainer

Waxed paper

Hand whisk

Electric mixer with whisk and paddle attachments

Candy thermometer

Heatproof spatula

Pastry bag with $^1\!/_2$-inch round tip (or new disposable pastry bag)

Cooling rack

Preheat the oven to 200°F (95°C). Stack 2 (18 x 13-inch) baking sheets on top of one another. Line the top baking sheet with a silicone mat or parchment paper. Cut additional sheets of parchment paper, if using, at the dimensions of the baking sheet to pipe additional batches. Place a piping guide (see page 29) under the silicone mat or parchment paper.

To proceed with the **FRENCH MERINGUE METHOD**, turn to **PAGE 40**.

To proceed with the **ITALIAN MERINGUE METHOD**, turn to **PAGE 45**.

To proceed with the **SWISS MERINGUE METHOD**, turn to **PAGE 51**.

To proceed with **KATHRYN'S EASIEST FRENCH METHOD**, turn to **PAGE 55**.

SUMMARY OF BAKING TIMES BY SIZE

MINIS ($\frac{1}{2}$ inch or 1 centimeter): 200°F (105°C) for 15 minutes. Increase the heat to 350°F (175°C) and bake for another 6 minutes.

SMALL (1 inch or 3 centimeters): 200°F (105°C) for 15 minutes. Increase the heat to 350°F (175°C) and bake for another 9 minutes.

LARGE (2 inches or 6 centimeters): 200°F (105°C) for 15 minutes. Increase the heat to 350°F (175°C) and bake for another 9 minutes. Reduce the heat to 300°F (150°C) and bake for 7 to 8 more minutes.

IN ALL FILLING PAIRING SUGGESTIONS, these unflavored shells are referred to as Almond Shells.

BASE MACARON RECIPE:

French Meringue Method

F rench meringue is the most basic of meringue methods, the one you probably used before if you've made angel food cake or meringue cookies. The sugar is not heated, but rather is whisked with the egg whites. It takes slightly longer for the meringue to form but does not require a candy thermometer. Many pastry chefs make their French meringue by gradually adding the sugar once the soft peak stage is reached. I have found that this can sometimes make for a looser meringue, causing the shells to spread, so I prefer adding the sugar at the beginning of the whipping process. It can reduce the volume capacity of the egg whites, but makes for a firmer meringue, and makes it more difficult for the novice baker to overwhip it. Because this type of shell is more prone to spreading, I add powdered egg whites to strengthen the protein structure.

THE BEFORE YOU BAKE SECTION, pages 24 to 33, includes detailed techniques for all the steps of the mixing, piping, baking, cooling, filling, and storing processes. Troubleshooting information is on pages 249 to 256.

1¼ packed cups (165 grams) almond flour

¾ packed cup (165 grams) confectioners' sugar

Pinch fine sea salt

1 tablespoon (5 grams) powdered egg white

¾ cup (150 grams) granulated sugar

½ cup (115 grams) aged egg whites (from 4 eggs; see page 19)

½ teaspoon (3 grams) cream of tartar

4 drops (gel) or 6 drops (liquid) food coloring (optional)

AFTER SETTING UP FOR BAKING (page 38), place the almond flour, confectioners' sugar, and salt in the bowl of a food processor and pulse 4 times for 3 seconds each to combine them. Scrape the sides of the bowl in between pulses with a spatula. Sift with a fine-mesh strainer onto a sheet of waxed paper. (If you simply sift the flour and sugar together without processing them first, the macaron will not be as smooth-skinned.)

MAKING THE FRENCH MERINGUE

With a hand whisk, whisk together the powdered egg whites and granulated sugar in the bowl of an electric mixer. Whisk in the egg whites and cream of tartar until the mixture is homogenous.

Set the bowl and whisk attachment on the mixer and whisk on medium speed until the meringue is glossy and forms stiff peaks, about 11 minutes.

Once the meringue reaches stiff peaks (the whisk will leave marks in the meringue as it goes around in the bowl) and resembles marshmallow fluff, stop the mixer. Turn the bowl upside down to check that you have reached the right stage: the meringue should not slip in the bowl (see photo below).

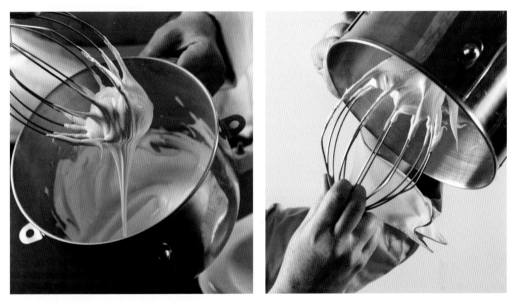

MACARONNER *(incorporating the ingredients)*

With a spatula, quickly fold the sifted dry ingredients into the meringue (see page 28 and photo page 44). If using food coloring, stop folding when the batter appears to be 90 percent incorporated, scrape the sides of the bowl, and fold in the desired coloring with 1 to 2 more strokes.

To pipe, bake, and fill the finished shells, follow the instructions on page 59.

FRENCH MERINGUE METHOD

BASE MACARON RECIPE:
Italian Meringue Method

italian meringue is the strongest of the three methods presented here because it creates the most stable and consistent structure for the macaron shells. If you've made shells with a French meringue and they spread too much, or you think that the Swiss meringue is too stiff to pipe, try this method. As the sugar syrup cooks to the soft-ball stage, the water evaporates. The syrup continues to cook, even off the heat, as it is slowly and steadily drizzled into the egg whites. It thus cooks the egg whites, resulting in a very strong protein structure. Italian meringue-based shells don't spread as much, for that reason. Because the sugar is fully melted into the batter, they also have the highest shine.

THE BEFORE YOU BAKE SECTION, pages 24 to 33, includes detailed techniques for all the steps of the mixing, piping, baking, cooling, filling, and storing processes. Troubleshooting information is on pages 249 to 256.

1¼ packed cups (165 grams) almond flour
¾ packed cup (165 grams) confectioners' sugar
Pinch fine sea salt
½ cup (115 grams) aged egg whites (from 4 eggs; see page 19)
½ teaspoon (3 grams) cream of tartar
¾ cup (150 grams) granulated sugar
4 drops (gel) or 6 drops (liquid) food coloring (optional)

AFTER SETTING UP FOR BAKING (page 38), place the almond flour, confectioners' sugar, and salt in the bowl of a food processor and pulse 4 times for 3 seconds each to combine them. Scrape the sides of the bowl in between pulses with a spatula. Sift with a fine-mesh strainer onto a sheet of waxed paper. (If you simply sift the flour and sugar together without processing them first, the macaron will not be as smooth-skinned.)

MAKING THE ITALIAN MERINGUE

In the bowl of an electric mixer fitted with the whisk attachment, begin to whisk the egg whites and cream of tartar on medium speed until soft peaks form, about 2 minutes. Reduce the speed to low if the egg whites are at soft peaks before the syrup is ready.

 While the egg whites are whipping, heat the granulated sugar and $^1\!/_4$ cup (57 grams) of water in a small saucepan over medium-high heat. Stir to dissolve the sugar. If sugar crystals stick to the edges of the pan, use a small pastry brush dipped in water to remove them. Clip a candy thermometer to the pan and cook until the sugar reaches 235°F (113°C), closely monitoring it. If using food coloring, add it to the syrup at 230°F (110°C).

ITALIAN MERINGUE METHOD

THE MERINGUE DOESN'T HAVE TO COOL COMPLETELY before you begin folding; in fact, the shells may form their skin better if you start with a slightly warm meringue.

When the sugar syrup reaches 235°F (113°C), quickly and steadily pour the syrup down the side of the mixer bowl, with the mixer running at medium speed. Rest the lip of the saucepan on the side of the bowl so the sugar does not hit the whisk attachment and splatter (it should run gradually down the side of the bowl). Continue whisking until stiff peaks form and the meringue is lukewarm and glossy, about 4 minutes. Do not overwhip the meringue or the feet of the macarons may not form correctly. Turn the bowl upside down to check that you have reached the right stage: the meringue should not slip in the bowl (see photo, opposite page).

NOTE: Once it reaches the right temperature, the syrup will be bubbling (large and small bubbles) throughout the entire surface of the pan. If you do not own a candy thermometer, check the temperature by dropping a few drops of syrup into ice water. The syrup should feel a bit sticky and form a soft ball in the water. This is also called the soft-ball test or stage.

MACARONNER *(incorporating the ingredients)*

Place the sifted dry ingredients in a large mixing bowl and push them toward the sides to form a well in the center of the bowl. Spoon the lukewarm meringue into the center. With a rubber spatula, stir the meringue from the center out in a circular motion, as if you were making pasta dough. The meringue will pick up the dry ingredients from the inside to the outside of the bowl; this process should take about 1 minute. Finish with 6 to 8 J-folds (see page 28).

To pipe, bake, and fill the finished shells, follow the instructions on page 59.

Swiss Meringue Method

If you've made boiled icing, or "seven-minute frosting," this type of meringue will sound familiar. It consists of whipping the egg whites and sugar over simmering water until they reach 130°F (55°C), and then folding in the dry ingredients. Heating the egg whites gives some strength to the meringue's protein structure, so that the batter will not be too loose. The batter will be stiffer than one made with French or Italian meringue bases, so make sure that you squeeze firmly when piping the shells.

THE BEFORE YOU BAKE SECTION, pages 24 to 33, includes detailed techniques for all the steps of the mixing, piping, baking, cooling, filling, and storing processes. Troubleshooting information is on pages 249 to 256.

MAKES 80 SMALL (1-INCH) SHELLS,
ENOUGH FOR 40 SANDWICHED MACARONS

1¼ packed cups (165 grams) almond flour
¾ packed cup (165 grams) confectioners' sugar
Pinch fine sea salt
½ cup (115 grams) aged egg whites (from 4 eggs; see page 19)
½ teaspoon (3 grams) cream of tartar
¾ cup (150 grams) granulated sugar
4 drops (gel) or 6 drops (liquid) food coloring (optional)

AFTER SETTING UP FOR BAKING (page 38), place the almond flour, confectioners' sugar, and salt in the bowl of a food processor and pulse 4 times for 3 seconds each to combine them. Scrape the sides of the bowl in between pulses with a spatula. Sift with a fine-mesh strainer onto a sheet of waxed paper. (If you simply sift the flour and sugar together without processing them first, the macaron will not be as smooth-skinned.)

MAKING THE SWISS MERINGUE

Fill a pot over which the bowl of your electric mixer can fit without touching the bottom with about 2 inches of water. Bring the water to a boil over high heat, then reduce the heat only slightly so the water is still boiling but flame or steam will not burn your arm. If the water is not hot enough, it will take too long for the meringue to form and the batter will be too thick and viscous to form beautiful macarons.

Put the egg whites, granulated sugar, and cream of tartar in the bowl of an electric mixer. With a hand whisk, whisk together to combine, then place the bowl over the lightly boiling

water. Clip a candy thermometer to the bowl, then whisk vigorously until the mixture reaches 130°F (55°C), 1 to 2 minutes.

NOTE: If you do not own a candy thermometer, insert a clean finger into the center of the mixture while you are whipping it (do not touch the bottom or sides of the bowl). When the egg whites and sugar reach 130°F (55°C), it will feel like extremely hot bath water to your finger.

Take the bowl off the heat, using a dry towel because it will be hot, and place it on the mixer. Fit the whisk attachment, and whisk at medium speed until glossy stiff peaks form, about 6 minutes. Turn the bowl upside down to check that you have reached the right stage: the meringue should not slip in the bowl (see photo belo).

MACARONNER *(incorporating the ingredients)*

Turn the mixer off and switch to the paddle attachment. Pour the sifted dry ingredients all at once into the bowl of the mixer. Beat on low to medium speed until all the ingredients are incorporated, about 20 seconds. If using food coloring, stop the mixer when the batter appears to be 90 percent incorporated, scrape the sides of the bowl with a spatula, and fold in the desired coloring with 2 to 3 strokes by hand (or 10 more seconds on the mixer).

To pipe, bake, and fill the finished shells, follow the instructions on page 59.

Because Swiss meringue is the stiffest of all three and might result in more tails on the shells, the "squeeze out and refill" tip to use before piping the full batch of macarons might be most necessary here.

BASE MACARON RECIPE:

Kathryn's Easiest French Macaron Method

Try the Easiest French method when you are pressed for time or when baking with kids. The results are very rewarding: These shells turn out just as beautiful (if a little flatter) and tasty as those made with traditional methods. The only downside is that they need to bake a few minutes longer or they will be too chewy. This method works best for one-inch shells (don't try it with larger ones, which won't form good feet) baked on a silicone mat rather than parchment paper.

THE EASIEST MACARON

COMPILING ALL THE TRICKS AND TIPS THAT I LEARNED OVER THE YEARS for this book made me think a lot about the theory behind macarons. Some sources say that they leaven with air, which never made sense to me because of the unusually long amount of time the macaronnage stage takes, compared to cakes leavened by air, such as angel food cake or genoise. Much of the air added during the process is removed when whipping the meringue to glossy peaks. Slamming the baking sheets before baking macarons also removes air pockets. I concluded that steam (as the water contained in the egg whites—about 90 percent of their structure—evaporates) plays just as major, if not greater, role as a leavener.

Applying standard baking theory based on other products that rise with steam (cream puffs, for example), I was able to develop this reliable method, which does not require actually making any meringue.

THE BEFORE YOU BAKE SECTION, pages 24 to 33, includes detailed techniques for all the steps of the mixing, piping, baking, cooling, filling, and storing processes. Troubleshooting information is on pages 249 to 256.

MAKES 80 SMALL (1-INCH) MACARONS,
ENOUGH FOR 40 SANDWICHED MACARONS

1¼ packed cups (165 grams) almond flour
¾ packed cup (165 grams) confectioners' sugar
Pinch fine sea salt
¾ cup (150 grams) granulated sugar
1 tablespoon (5 grams) powdered egg white
½ cup (115 grams) fresh unaged egg whites (from 4 eggs, see note page 58)
4 drops (gel) or 6 drops (liquid) food coloring (optional)

After setting up for baking (page 38), place the almond flour, confectioners' sugar, and salt in the bowl of a food processor and pulse 4 times for 3 seconds each to combine them. Scrape the sides of the bowl in between pulses with a spatula. Add the granulated sugar and powdered egg white, and repeat the pulsing 4 more times. Sift with a fine-mesh strainer into a medium bowl. (If you simply sift the flour and sugar together without processing them first, the macaron will not be as smooth-skinned.)

MAKING THE EASIEST BATTER

Pour the egg whites all at once into the almond flour mixture, and stir with a rubber spatula until everything is just combined, in 8 to 10 strokes. If using food coloring, when the batter appears to be 90 percent incorporated, fold in the desired coloring. Continue to mix only until the batter appears homogenous, at most 30 seconds.

Cover the batter with plastic wrap placed directly over it (not on top of the bowl), to prevent a skin from forming, and let the batter sit 1 hour at room temperature. It will be thick, but loosen somewhat in the hour.

To pipe, bake, and fill the finished shells, follow the instructions on page 59.

NOTE: When ready to make the batter, separate the 4 egg whites and pour them into a bowl or a glass. Whisk them lightly to break them up, then measure the exact amount needed for the recipe (you will have just a little bit of egg white leftover).

Baking

PIPING AND BAKING MACARON SHELLS

Spoon the batter in a pastry bag fitted with a $\frac{1}{2}$-inch round tip (alternatively, cut a $\frac{1}{2}$-inch opening in the bag). Fill the bag halfway, leaving the rest of the meringue in the bowl while piping; cover it with plastic wrap while a batch is in the oven. If you overfill the bag, you will not be able to squeeze it hard enough in order to pipe even, tail-less shells. Twist the top of the bag to close.

Pipe the meringue on the silicone mat or parchment-lined baking sheet into quarter-size mounds, 1½ inches apart from one another. Holding the tip of the bag at a 90-degree angle ¼-inch above the baking sheet, firmly squeeze it until the batter fills the circle on the piping guide and is about ¼-inch high. Do not move the bag while squeezing out the batter. As soon as you have reached the desired size, completely release the pressure on the bag and twist your wrist in a clockwise direction, without lifting it up. Once the batter stops flowing, stop squeezing the bag, lift, and move onto the next circle on the piping guide. Prolonged pressure on the batter and/or quick lifting results in "tails" (or peaks) on the shell, which might not settle out.

Pipe a test shell or two to double-check the viscosity of the batter. Firmly slam the baking sheets down to remove excess air and see if the three-dimensional tails settle out, lifting the sheets about 6 inches above the table, about 6 times (you may see some air bubbles rise). Don't be afraid to really slam them. If the tails do not settle and the

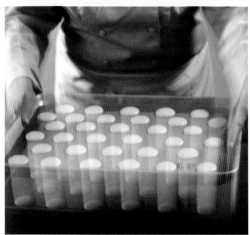

surface of the macaron is not smooth, squeeze the batter back into the bowl, then immediately refill the pastry bag. Continue piping, then slam the baking sheets again. This eliminates excess air or stiffness from the batter without requiring additional folding (which can cause cracking). Slide out the piping guide to use again.

Bake the French, Italian, and Swiss meringue shells at 200°F (95°C) for 15 minutes to dry out the shells. Increase the oven temperature to 350°F (175°C) and bake for an additional 9 minutes, until the foot and edge of the shells feel firm and they just come off the parchment paper if you forcibly lift them. For Kathryn's Easiest French shells, bake at 200°F (95°C) for 15 minutes. Increase the temperature to 350°F (175°C) and bake for an additional 11 minutes, rotating after 6 minutes. Check that the center of the shells are risen; if they have any slight indentation, appear to be darker in their centers, or have a wrinkled skin after 11
minutes, reduce the heat to 300°F (150°C) and continue baking for up to 5 more minutes. Bake until the feet of the shell feel firm and the shells can just come off the parchment paper if you lift them.

If the shells are darkening too quickly, put a wooden spoon in the door of the oven to prop it slightly open and lessen the heat. If you do not use food coloring, the macarons should remain very pale, and not turn golden. While that first batch of macarons bakes, keep any remaining batter in the pastry bag to pipe additional batches.

Your oven will not truly be 350°F (175°C) when you raise the temperature—it takes time to reach that from the initial 200°F (95°C). The increase in heat that takes place as the oven makes its way toward 350°F (175°C) is, however, enough to bake the shells.

Remove the shells from the oven and lower the oven temperature to 200°F (95°C). Slide the silicone mat or parchment paper onto a cooling rack and let the shells cool completely, about 1 hour. Pipe and bake the next pan.

FILLING

To fill the cooled shells, turn them over, so that their flat side faces you. Pipe the filling on half the shells, in mounds about $\frac{1}{2}$-inch high, leaving $\frac{1}{4}$ inch to the edges. Place another shell of matching size flat-side down onto the filling to make a sandwich. Twist lightly to sandwich them together securely. Store them in an airtight container in the refrigerator for up to three days, or freeze them for up to three weeks.

SWEET SHELLS

WALNUT ✶ PECAN ✶ HAZELNUT

CASHEW ✶ MACADAMIA

✶ COCONUT ✶ PISTACHIO ✶ VANILLA

COCOA ✶ *Variations: Cocoa with Cocoa Nibs;*

Red Velvet ✶ ESPRESSO ✶ ORANGE ✶

LIME ✶ LEMON-POPPYSEED ✶

Variation: Lemon ✶ LICORICE ✶ MINT

✶ BLACKBERRY ✶ STRAWBERRY ✶

PASSION FRUIT ✶ CINNAMON

✶ CARDAMOM ✶ FIVE-SPICE ✶

GINGER ✶ GREEN TEA ✶ MARIGOLD

✶ LAVENDER ✶ ROSE ✶ VIOLET

Macaron shells with no flavoring or color added are not plain: They have a wonderful almond taste that make them delectable on their own, especially early on as you make your first batches and get familiar with the process. You will soon want to experiment and expand your assortment of shells, however. The following recipes offer an array of flavors and colors with which you can play. The proportions are enough to flavor one full batch of your favorite base method, to make 80 small one-inch shells, or 40 sandwiched macarons.

FOOD COLORINGS EXIST AS FOOD-SAFE LIQUIDS, gels, pastes, or powders. Liquids contain more water, so use them sparingly when coloring macarons: Too much liquid can cause crispness and cracking. If you use gel food colors rather than liquid ones, reduce the amount given in the recipes by one drop. When using powdered coloring, be careful to not add more than indicated, as they can leave an undesirable aftertaste when used in excess. Start with ½ teaspoon (.5 gram) and add more if necessary. Certain colors might affect how the batter spreads. If you notice that it spreads too much when piping a test shell, pipe smaller shells.

MAKE YOUR OWN NUT FLOUR

IF GROUND FOR TOO LONG, NUTS TURN INTO PASTE BECAUSE OF THEIR high oil content. Home equipment, like a food processor, often lacks the power to rapidly turn whole nuts into nut flour. But it is possible and you will achieve good results for these recipes by starting with whole nuts and using a few tips.

* If the nuts were stored in the refrigerator or freezer, bring them to room temperature. Make sure that they are not wet or cold before proceeding.

* Coarsely chop the nuts with a chef's knife.

* Place the chopped nuts in the bowl of a food processor and pulse for 3 seconds at a time so that they don't get too warm and turn into a paste. Pulse about 30 times.

* Scrape the sides of the bowl in between every 4 pulses with a rubber spatula so that no nuts stick to the sides and all the nuts grind evenly.

* When the nuts have turned into a fine flour, sift them onto a piece of waxed paper. Measure to ensure that you have enough nuts for the recipe. If not, repeat the above steps.

* Preheat the oven to 200°F (95°C) and spread the ground nuts on a baking sheet. Dry them in the oven for 30 minutes, then let them cool completely.

* Proceed with the recipe as written. Grinding the resulting flour with the confectioners' sugar will ensure that it is fine enough, even if it was still a bit coarse when coming out of the oven.

YOU CAN SUCCESSFULLY SUBSTITUTE GROUND WALNUTS, PECANS, hazelnuts (blanched or with their skins for a more rustic effect), cashews, macadamias, or shredded and dried coconut for the whole amount of almond flour in any of the base recipes. The texture and flavor will be similar to macarons made with almond flour if you grind the nuts finely enough, with undertones specific to each nut. In order to obtain the required amount of nut flour, begin with the following amounts of whole nuts:

$1^1/_2$ cups (165 grams) whole walnuts
$1^1/_2$ cups (165 grams) whole pecans
1 cup plus 2 tablespoons (165 grams) whole hazelnuts
1 heaping cup plus 1 tablespoon (165 grams) whole cashews
1 heaping cup plus 1 tablespoon (165 grams) whole macadamias
$2^1/_4$ cups (165 grams) dried unsweetened flaked coconut

For instructions on grinding your own nuts, see page 67.

IMAGE ON RIGHT: *Macadamia Shells with Ginger Cream*

Pistachio flour is also available commer-cially through wholesalers (see Resources, page 257). You can substitute pistachio flour for the almond flour in your favorite base recipe (see page 34). These pale green shells pair well with Crunchy Cocoa Nib Ganache (page 107).

Pistachio

1½ cups (165 grams) whole pistachios,
   finely ground into a flour (see page 67)

3 drops liquid green food coloring

2 drops liquid yellow food coloring

40 pistachios, shelled (optional)

Prepare your favorite base recipe (page 34), substituting pistachio flour for the almond flour. Fold in the food coloring at the macaronnage stage.

   If desired, top half of the shells with 1 pistachio nut immediately after piping them.

IMAGE ON LEFT: *Pistachio Shells with Crunchy Cacao Nib Ganache*

These macarons are not only perfumed with *vanilla, they also become speckled, thanks to the seeds of the vanilla bean. They are perhaps the most ubiquitous flavor of shells, other than the simple almond ones, and can be paired with nearly all the fillings in this book. You can create a dramatic color contrast with the bright purple Cassis-White Chocolate Ganache (page 124).*

Vanilla

1 vanilla bean

Split the vanilla bean in half lengthwise, and use the back of a paring knife to scrape out the seeds. Stir them into the granulated sugar used for the base recipe, and rub the bean into the sugar to extract as many seeds as possible. Proceed with your favorite base recipe (page 34).

IMAGE ON RIGHT: *Vanilla Shells with Orange Cream*

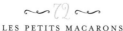

Cocoa macarons need to bake 2 minutes

longer than the base recipe directs. Try them with Basil Buttercream (page 136) or Rosemary Caramel (page 162).

1 packed cup (145 grams) almond flour
²/₃ packed cup (145 grams) confectioners' sugar
¼ cup (25 grams) Dutch-process cocoa powder

Cocoa

Place the almond flour, confectioners' sugar, and cocoa powder in the bowl of a food processor and pulse 4 times for 3 seconds each to combine them. Scrape the sides of the bowl in between pulses with a spatula. Sift with a fine-mesh strainer onto a sheet of waxed paper, then proceed with your favorite base recipe (page 34) as directed. The batter will appear stiff; let it sit for 1 hour, covered, before piping and baking. Bake the shells for an extra 2 minutes.

NOTE: Since cocoa powder bakes differently than nut flours do, first try these shells with the French meringue method. With practice, they can be made with all three meringue methods.

Variation: Cocoa with Cacao Nibs

Cacao nibs are crumbled pieces of the cacao bean, and have a sophisticated, almost bitter flavor. They are available in specialty grocery stores and online (see Resources, page 257).

Top half of the shells with a few cocoa nibs (2 tablespoons [18 grams] total) before baking.

IMAGE ON LEFT: *Cocoa Shells with Basil Buttercream*

Variation: Red Velvet

Use these to make Red Velvet Cake Macarons (page 208), but you can also fill them with buttercreams or ice milks.

Reduce the amount of cocoa powder to 2 tablespoons plus 1$\frac{1}{2}$ teaspoons (17.5 grams) and add 5 drops of red liquid food coloring (4 drops if using gel) at the macaronnage stage.

A few drops of yellow food coloring (see

page 21) turns the macaron shells a light brown and hints at its caffeinated flavor. Do not use instant coffee, but rather the instant espresso powder that is available on most supermarket aisles. It has a more concentrated flavor and a much finer texture. Fill the macarons with Cinnamon Cappuccino Ganache (page 108).

Espresso

1 tablespoon (5 grams) espresso powder
2 drops liquid yellow food coloring

Add the espresso powder to the almond flour and confectioners' sugar once they are sifted. Proceed with your favorite base recipe (page 34).

Fold in the food coloring at the macaronnage stage.

Some of my favorite pairings for this fla-vored shell are *Orange Cream (page 145), Earl Grey Ganache (page 123), Apricot-Ginger-Chocolate Caramel (page 170), and Duck Confit with Port and Figs (page 234). Using orange oil will give the macarons more of a zip than zest will, but either option is fine.*

1 packed teaspoon (4 grams) finely grated orange zest
(from ½ orange) or ¼ teaspoon (1 gram) orange oil
4 drops orange liquid food coloring

Prepare your favorite base recipe (page 34).
Fold in the zest and food coloring at the macaronnage stage.

Orange

JUICING AND ZESTING CITRUS

BECAUSE THE FRUITS' SIZES CAN VARY ENORMOUSLY, quantities are given in tablespoons and by weight, to be as accurate as possible; the approximate equivalent in whole fruits appears in parentheses to help you shop. It's always a good idea to buy at least one more than needed, in case the fruits are not very juicy.

Use a Microplane zester to finely grate citrus zest, and measure it by packing it in a teaspoon or tablespoon, if not weighing. Use a vegetable peeler to remove strips of the peel, and avoid cutting into the white pith, which is bitter.

Lime

Other than Key Lime with Marshmallow *(page 212), these shells are perfect for Chile-Pineapple-Kumquat Marmalade (page 196) or Buttermilk Ice Milk (page 178).*

1 packed teaspoon (4 grams) finely grated lime zest
(from 1 lime) or ¼ teaspoon (1 gram) lime oil

Prepare your favorite base recipe (page 34).
Fold in the lime zest at the macaronnage stage.

Lemon-Poppyseed

Try these paired with Lemon Curd *(page 149) or Lemon-Almond Cream (page 157).*

1 packed teaspoon (4 grams) finely grated lemon zest
(from 1 lemon) or ¼ teaspoon (1 gram) lemon oil
5 drops liquid yellow food coloring
2 tablespoons (18 grams) poppy seeds

Prepare your favorite base recipe (page 34).
Fold in the lemon zest and food coloring at the macaronnage stage.
After piping the macarons, evenly sprinkle a few poppy seeds on top of half the shells and bake as directed.

Variation: Lemon

Omit the poppyseeds for a plain lemon flavor.

This shell has a beautiful, dramatic jet-black

color that will further deepen if you let the batter sit, covered, for 30 minutes before piping the shells. I like to pair it with a simple Vanilla Buttercream (page 131) or Pear Cream (page 148), for contrasting color effects. For true licorice lovers, pair it with Anise Ice Milk (page 177).

1½ teaspoons (1.5 grams) powdered black food coloring

3 tablespoons (60 grams) licorice flavor compound or
¼ teaspoon (1 gram) anise oil

Licorice

Prepare your favorite base recipe (page 34), pulsing the powdered coloring in the food processor with the other dry ingredients.

Fold in the licorice compound at the macaronnage stage.

Mint

This bright green shell pairs well with gan-
aches (pages 104 to 127, particularly with Chocolate-Mint), as well as Fudgesicle Ice Milk (page 179).

3 tablespoons (60 grams) mint flavor compound or
¼ teaspoon (1 gram) mint oil
4 drops liquid mint green food coloring

Prepare your favorite base recipe (page 34).
 Fold in the mint compound at the macaronnage stage.

FLAVOR COMPOUNDS

DO NOT SUBSTITUTE EXTRACTS FOR THE FLAVOR COM- pounds. Extracts are water based and would add too much liquid to the macaron base.

Pair these shells with Pistachio Buttercream

(page 134), Blackberry Jelly (page 198), or Lemon Curd (page 149).

Blackberry

3 tablespoons (60 grams) blackberry flavor compound
3 drops liquid purple food coloring
1 drop liquid blue food coloring

Prepare your favorite base recipe (page 34).

   Fold in the blackberry compound and food colorings at the macaronnage stage.

Strawberry

For the ultimate ice cream macaron, pair these with *Almond Ice Milk (page 176). Vanilla Buttercream (page 131) also works well, as does Strawberry-Guava Pâte de Fruit (page 200).*

3 tablespoons (60 grams) strawberry flavor compound
3 drops liquid pink food coloring

Prepare your favorite base recipe (page 34).
   Fold in the strawberry compound and food coloring at the macaronnage stage.

Try these shells with Apricot–Passion Pâte
de Fruit (page 199) and Passion Fruit Pastry Cream (page 155).

Passion Fruit

      3 tablespoons (60 grams) passion fruit flavor compound

      4 drops liquid egg yellow food coloring

Prepare your favorite base recipe (page 34).

    Fold in the passion fruit compound and food coloring at the macaronnage stage.

Cinnamon

Cinnamon is one of the most beloved flavors *in American baked goods. I like to keep things traditional and use these shells with fillings such as Cinnamon-Apple Butter with Calvados (page 187) or Oatmeal Cookie Buttercream (page 141).*

2½ teaspoons (7 grams) ground cinnamon

Sift the cinnamon with the almond flour and confectioners' sugar, then proceed with your favorite base recipe (page 34).

Cardamom

Enhance the cardamom flavor of these shells *with fillings such as Vanilla Buttercream (page 131) or Chai Ganache (page 119).*

2 teaspoons (5 grams) ground cardamom

Sift the cardamom with the almond flour and confectioners' sugar, then proceed with your favorite base recipe (page 34).

Pear Cream (page 148), Crunchy Cacao Nib

Ganache (page 107), or Maple Buttercream (page 133) are among the fillings I most like to pair with these shells.

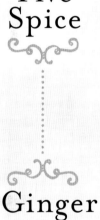

Five Spice

2 teaspoons (5 grams) Chinese 5-spice powder

Sift the spice powder with the almond flour and confectioners' sugar, then proceed with your favorite base recipe (page 34).

Use these shells with the Thai-Chile-Peanut

filling (page 225) or Gingerbread Buttercream (page 144).

Ginger

1 tablespoon (6 grams) ground ginger

Sift the ginger with the almond flour and confectioners' sugar, then proceed with your favorite base recipe (page 34).

Green Tea

Green tea powder is sold as matcha in tea *shops around the country and online (see Resources, page 257). It has a pale green color and an herbal taste that mellows out when distributed throughout the almond flour and sugar. Pair these shells with Green Tea and White Chocolate Ganache (page 115), Sesame Buttercream (page 139), or Almond Ice Milk (page 176).*

1½ teaspoons (3 grams) matcha powder
3 drops liquid green food coloring

Sift the matcha powder with the almond flour and confectioners' sugar, then proceed with your favorite base recipe (page 34).

Fold in the food coloring at the macaronnage stage.

IMAGE ON RIGHT: *Green Tea Shells with Vanilla Buttercream*

If you grow marigolds and do not use pesticides on them, they will be perfect for cooking. We have never seen them available commercially, unlike rose petals and lavender flowers, so this recipe is best suited to gardeners—or their friends. You can use other types of organically grown flowers as long as you ensure that they are edible. What's Cooking America (www.whatscookingamerica.net) offers a complete list of edible plants. Pair them with Vanilla Buttercream (page 131), Orange-Buttermilk Ice Milk (page 178), or Orange Cream (page 145).

Marigold

2 tablespoons (3 grams) organically grown marigold petals, finely chopped

4 drops liquid yellow food coloring

Prepare your favorite base recipe (page 34).

Fold in the marigold petals and food coloring at the macaronnage stage.

If you have more petals available, top half of the shells with a petal after piping and bake as directed.

These macarons look even prettier if only
*one lavender blossom is placed on each shell. Use tweezers—and a bit of
patience—to arrange them individually at the center of the shell. Lavender
has a very strong, flowery taste, so it takes very little of it to perfume an
entire batch of macarons. You can buy organic edible lavender online (see
Resources, page 257) if your local garden store doesn't carry it; only use
culinary-quality lavender, not the type sold in craft stores. Pair these shells
with Blackberry Jelly (page 198) or Earl Grey Ganache (page 123).*

Lavender

> 2 teaspoons (1 gram) dried, organically grown
> lavender blossoms, divided
> 5 drops liquid light purple food coloring

In a spice grinder, grind 1 teaspoon lavender to a very fine powder.

Prepare your favorite base recipe. Fold in the ground lavender and food
coloring at the macaronnage stage (page 34).

After piping the macarons, evenly sprinkle the remaining whole lavender
blossoms on top of half the shells, placing one per shell if desired. Bake as
directed.

You can buy organic edible rose petals on-line (see *Resources, page 257*) *if your local garden store doesn't carry them, or you can use your own roses if you garden without pesticides. Do not use petals sold in craft stores, which are not of culinary quality. Pluck the petals and spread them on a towel to dry for about 10 days. While it has a pronounced herbal flavor, this shell is more versatile than you might imagine. It pairs well with most ganaches, frozen fillings, and fruit fillings.*

1 packed tablespoon (1 gram) dried organically
grown rose petals, finely chopped
5 drops liquid pink food coloring

Prepare your favorite base recipe (page 34).
Fold in the rose petals and food coloring at the macaronnage stage.

IMAGE ON LEFT: *Rose Shells with Rose-Raspberry Ganache*

Rose

Violet

These purple shells pair well with Vanilla
*Buttercream (page 131). You can also accentuate the flowery effect with
Rose-Raspberry Ganache (page 110), and top half of the shells with candied violet petals before baking. You can find those in specialty baking
stores and most gourmet grocery stores.*

3 tablespoons (60 grams) violet flavor compound
4 drops liquid purple food coloring

Prepare your favorite base recipe (page 34).
Fold in the violet compound and food coloring at the macaronnage stage.

IMAGE ON RIGHT: *Violet Shells with Cassis-White Chocolate Ganache*

SAVORY SHELLS

PARSLEY ✻ **SAFFRON** ✻
PINK PEPPERCORN ✻ *Variation: Black Pepper*
✻ **ANCHO CHILE** ✻ **SESAME** ✻
WASABI

Macarons are no longer sweet-only treats, and with a little imagination, they can be paired with fillings that contain meat, vegetables, or cheese. But these savory shells work with sweet fillings, too, allowing for some truly creative combinations. Dare to experiment: try a buttercream filling in a saffron shell, an ice milk in an ancho chile shell, or a luxurious ganache to temper the heat of a wasabi shell.

Follow a base recipe with the proper modifications (see below), and add your favorite flavor from the ones listed here. The proportions are enough to flavor one full batch of your favorite base method, to make 80 small one-inch shells, or 40 sandwiched macarons.

SAVORY SHELL VARIATION

SAVORY SHELLS WORK BEST WITH SMALL (1-INCH) MACARONS, because the slight decrease in the sugar modifies the stability of the meringue (smaller macarons are easier to bake). Follow your favorite base recipe (pages 34 to 58), decreasing the granulated sugar to $\frac{1}{2}$ cup plus 2 tablespoons (130 grams) and increasing the fine sea salt to $\frac{1}{4}$ teaspoon (1 gram).

The ideal ingredient to make these parsley *macarons is a parsley powder sold by Atlantic Spice (see Resources, page 257). Dried parsley will work as well if you first grind it to a powder in a spice grinder. Use these shells with Foie Gras with Black Currant Gastrique (page 231).*

> 1 tablespoon (6 grams) ground dried parsley

Sift the ground parsley with the almond flour and confectioners' sugar, then proceed with your favorite base recipe (page 34), decreasing the granulated sugar to $\frac{1}{2}$ cup plus 2 tablespoons (130 grams) and increasing the fine sea salt to $\frac{1}{4}$ teaspoon (1 gram).-Rosemary

IMAGE ON LEFT: *Parsley and Pink Peppercorn Shells with Chèvre Rosemary*

Parsley

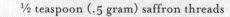

Saffron

These shells are beautifully adorned with *bright yellow speckles, thanks to the saffron. Use them with Tomato Confit (page 226) or Blood Orange Caramel (page 165).*

½ teaspoon (.5 gram) saffron threads

Gently stir the saffron into the sifted almond flour and confectioners' sugar, then proceed with your favorite base recipe (page 34), decreasing the granulated sugar to ½ cup plus 2 tablespoons (130 grams) and increasing the fine sea salt to ¼ teaspoon (1 gram).

IMAGE ON RIGHT: *Saffron Shells with Strawberry-Guava Pâte de Fruit*

*Try these paired with Chèvre-Rosemary
(page 222) for a savory twist, or White-Chocolate-Grapefruit Ganache
(page 116), for example.*

Pink Peppercorn

1 tablespoon (6 grams) whole pink peppercorns
4 drops liquid light pink food coloring

With a rolling pin, crush the peppercorns.

Prepare your favorite base recipe (page 34), decreasing the granulated sugar to $^1/_2$ cup plus 2 tablespoons (130 grams) and increasing the fine sea salt to $^1/_4$ teaspoon (1 gram).

Fold in 2 teaspoons (4 grams) crushed peppercorns and the food coloring at the macaronnage stage.

After piping the macarons, evenly sprinkle the remaining 1 teaspoon (2 grams) crushed peppercorns on top of half the shells. Bake as directed.

IMAGE ON LEFT: *Black Pepper Shells with Lemon-Star Anise Ganache*

Variation: Black Pepper

Substitute $^1/_2$ teaspoon coarsely ground black pepper and omit the food coloring. Fold all the pepper at the macaronnage stage. Pair them with Foie Gras with Black Currant Gastrique (page 231), Persimmon Ice Milk (page 181), Strawberry–Guava Pâte de Fruit (page 200) or White Peach Jam (page 192).

Ancho Chile

Use this shell with the Chicken Mole filling *(page 229) or Crunchy Cacao Nib Ganache (page 107)*.

½ teaspoon (.5 gram) ground ancho chile

Sift the ancho chile with the almond flour and confectioners' sugar, then proceed with your favorite base recipe (page 34), decreasing the granulated sugar to ¹/₂ cup plus 2 tablespoons (130 grams) and increasing the fine sea salt to ¹/₄ teaspoon (1 gram).

Sesame

We like using these shells with Hummus *(page 220), since they share a sesame flavor. They also are good paired with Sesame Buttercream (page 139) or Fleur de Sel Caramel (page 160)*.

1 tablespoon plus 1 teaspoon (12 grams) hulled sesame seeds
1 tablespoon plus 1 teaspoon (12 grams) black sesame seeds

Follow your favorite base recipe (page 34), decreasing the granulated sugar to ¹/₂ cup plus 2 tablespoons (130 grams) and increasing the fine sea salt to ¹/₄ teaspoon (1 gram).

After piping the macarons, evenly sprinkle a few sesame seeds of each kind on top of each shell. Bake as directed.

As you would expect from wasabi, these shells have a slow-rising spiciness to them that make them particularly fitted for chocolate fillings (pages 104 to 119), or very fresh ones, such as ice milks (pages 174 to 183). Fabian Rimann, the pastry chef/owner of Max Chocolatier in Lucerne, Switerzland, introduced this flavor combination to me one year at the World Pastry Championship, and I have been unable to it combination out of my head since. You will find wasabi powder in the Asian product aisle of gourmet food stores or online (see Resources, page 257).

Wasabi

2 ½ teaspoons (2.5 grams) wasabi powder

Sift the wasabi powder with the almond flour and confectioners' sugar, then proceed with your favorite base recipe (page 34), decreasing the granulated sugar to ½ cup plus 2 tablespoons (130 grams) and increasing the fine sea salt to ¼ teaspoon (1 gram).

GANACHE FILLINGS

CRUNCHY CACAO NIB ✦ CINNAMON CAPPUCCINO WITH

CHOCOLATE-CINNAMON CRUNCH ✦ ROSE-RASPBERRY ✦

CHOCOLATE-MINT ✦ *Variation: Chocolate-Tarragon* ✦

GREEN TEA AND WHITE CHOCOLATE ✦ WHITE

CHOCOLATE-GRAPEFRUIT ✦ LEMON-STAR ANISE

✦ CHAI ✦ LAPSANG SOUCHONG WITH WHISKEY ✦

Variation: Earl Grey ✦ CASSIS–WHITE CHOCOLATE ✦

CRUNCHY HAZELNUT GIANDUJA ✦

Variation: Peanut Gianduja

Ganache is the unctuous, smooth result of mixing cream with dark, milk, or even white chocolate. It can be flavored with a wide variety of ingredients, such as herbs, liqueurs, spices, and fruits. It often includes softened butter, for additional richness, or a sugar syrup for a more stable texture. There are many ways to make ganache. The recipes here make use of a food processor, to create the complete emulsion of the ingredients and the best possible texture for a macaron filling.

POURING GANACHES INTO A SHALLOW PAN allows them to cool faster. You can use a casserole dish or a cake pan. When ready to pipe, it will have the texture of peanut butter.

PIPING GANACHE

SPOON THE GANACHE INTO A PASTRY BAG AND CUT A ½-INCH OPEN-ing at the tip (or use a ½-inch tip). Pipe a small amount of ganache, about ½-inch thick, in a circular shape, on the flat sides of the shells. Don't let the ganache go all the way to the edges of the macaron. Top with another shell, twisting it slightly to secure the filling, and let set in the refrigerator, about 10 minutes.

Ganache will thicken as it cools, so pipe quickly.

Cacao nibs are tiny pieces of a roasted cacao
*bean. Their chocolate flavor is very pronounced—and unsweetened. Pair
this ganache with Wasabi (page 103), or Ancho Chile (page 102) shells.*

MAKES 1 PINT, ENOUGH FOR
40 SMALL SANDWICHED MACARONS

11 ounces (320 grams) semisweet chocolate, chopped

2 tablespoons (36 grams) light corn syrup

1 cup (240 grams) heavy cream

1 tablespoon (14 grams) unsalted butter,
   softened and cut into 4 pieces

3 tablespoons (27 grams) cacao nibs (Resources, page 257)

Crunchy Cacao Nib

Pulse the chocolate in a food processor to chop into small pieces.

Bring the corn syrup and cream to a boil in a small saucepan over medium-
high heat. Immediately pour it over the chocolate in the food processor. Wait
1 minute to let the chocolate melt completely, then pulse until the mixture is
completely smooth. Add the butter and pulse until it is completely incorporated and the ganache is homogeneous and shiny. Stir in the cacao nibs.

Pour the ganache into a shallow pan, and let it cool at room temperature
until it becomes pipeable, about 15 minutes, stirring occasionally. To check,
periodically use a small spoon to scoop out some of the ganache. If it holds a
ball-like shape, it is ready. This ganache can be kept covered and refrigerated for up to 2 weeks.

IMAGE ON LEFT: *Cinnamon Shells with Crunchy Cacao Nib Ganache*

Rather than using cocoa powder, I like to

sprinkle cinnamon on top of my cappuccino. It gives it a hint of sweetness that makes the drink feel more like a treat. Pair this ganache with Espresso (page 76), Cinnamon (page 84), or Cocoa (page 75) shells.

Cinnamon Cappuccino
with Chocolate-Cinnamon Crunch

Makes 1 pint, enough for 40 small sandwiched macarons

2 tablespoons (36 grams) light corn syrup

1 cup (240 grams) heavy cream

4 cinnamon sticks

½ teaspoon (1 gram) espresso powder

5½ ounces (160 grams) semisweet chocolate, chopped

5½ ounces (160 grams) milk chocolate, chopped

Chocolate-Cinnamon Crunch (recipe follows), optional

Bring the corn syrup, cream, cinnamon sticks, and espresso powder to a boil in a small saucepan over medium-high heat. Remove from the heat and let the cinnamon infuse for 1 hour.

Pulse the chocolate in a food processor to chop into small pieces.

Remove the cinnamon sticks from the cream, bring the mixture back to a boil over medium-high heat, and immediately pour it over the chocolate in the food processor. Wait 1 minute to let the chocolate melt completely, then pulse until the mixture is completely smooth, homogeneous, and shiny.

Pour the ganache into a shallow pan and stir in the chocolate-cinnamon

crunch if using. Let it cool at room temperature until it becomes pipeable, about 15 minutes, stirring occasionally. To check, periodically use a small spoon to scoop out some of the ganache. If it holds a ball-like shape, it is ready. This ganache can be kept covered and refrigerated for up to 2 weeks.

Chocolate–Cinnamon Crunch

½ cup (100 grams) granulated sugar
3 ounces (90 grams) semisweet chocolate, chopped
½ teaspoon (1.5 gram) ground cinnamon

Line a baking sheet with parchment paper.

Cook the sugar in a small saucepan over medium-high heat until it turns a clear amber color, the edges begin to foam, and you can smell the caramel, about 5 minutes. Stir only if the sugar does not melt evenly. Remove from the heat and quickly whisk in the chocolate and cinnamon.

Pour the caramel onto the baking sheet in a thin layer and let it cool completely until it is hard and cool, about 20 minutes. Break it into large pieces and add them to the bowl of a food processor. Process until the caramel is broken into even-sized crunchy bits, about 8 pulses. The crunch can be stored in an airtight container at room temperature for up to 1 month.

Rose and raspberry are a perfect summer *combination, when both might even abound in your garden. I don't grow raspberries, but some of my neighbors do and are always happy to share their bounty, especially if they get to enjoy some of the macarons afterward. Pair this filling with Rose (page 91) or Strawberry (page 82) shells. You can purchase raspberry purée and rose compound—a thicker flavoring agent—online (see Resources, page 257). You can also use frozen raspberries: let them thaw, then puree them and strain them through a fine-mesh strainer so that the purée is completely smooth. The strength of a compound can vary from one manufacturer to the next, so taste your ganache and add more compound (about $1/2$ teaspoon [3.5 grams] at a time) if you want a more pronounced flavor.*

Rose-Raspberry

MAKES 1 PINT, ENOUGH FOR 40 SMALL SANDWICHED MACARONS

11 ounces (320 grams) white chocolate, chopped

2 tablespoons (36 grams) light corn syrup

¾ cup (180 grams) sour cream

¼ cup (60 grams) raspberry purée

1 tablespoon (14 grams) unsalted butter, very soft

1 teaspoon (7 grams) rose compound

1 tablespoon (13 grams) framboise (raspberry eau de vie)

Put the chocolate in the bowl of a food processor and pulse several times until it is chopped into small pieces. Leave the chocolate in the processor.

Bring the corn syrup, cream, and raspberry purée to a boil in a small saucepan over medium-high heat. Immediately pour it over the chocolate in the food processor. Wait 1 minute to let the chocolate melt completely, then pulse until the mixture is completely smooth. With the food processor running, add the butter, then the rose compound, then the framboise, and pulse until everything is completely incorporated and the ganache is homogeneous and shiny.

Pour the ganache into a shallow pan, and let it cool at room temperature until it becomes pipeable, about 15 minutes, stirring occasionally. To check, periodically use a small spoon to scoop out some of the ganache. If it holds a ball-like shape, it is ready. This ganache can be kept covered and refrigerated for up to 2 weeks.

I prefer using mint leaves in a ganache rather *than extract; it gives it a more natural, fresh flavor. Pair it with Mint (page 80), Cocoa (page 75), or Lemon (page 78) shells. Around the holidays, I like to then roll the filled macarons in peppermint that I crush with a rolling pin (place in a bag first to avoid making a mess).*

Chocolate-Mint

MAKES 1 PINT, ENOUGH FOR
40 SMALL SANDWICHED MACARONS

1 cup (240 grams) heavy cream

2 tablespoons (36 grams) light corn syrup

1 loosely packed cup (10 grams) fresh mint leaves
   (from about 1 bunch)

5½ ounces (160 grams) semisweet chocolate, chopped

5½ ounces (160 grams) milk chocolate, chopped

1 tablespoon (14 grams) unsalted butter,
   softened and cut into 4 pieces

Bring the cream, corn syrup, and mint to a boil in a small saucepan over medium-high heat. Remove from the heat and let the mint infuse for 1 hour. Pour the mixture into a blender (or use an immersion blender directly in the pan) and blend until it is smooth, 1 minute.

Put the chocolate in the bowl of a food processor and pulse several times until it is chopped into small pieces. Leave the chocolate in the processor.

(continued)

IMAGE ON LEFT: *Mint Shells with Chocolate-Mint Ganache and crushed peppermint*

Bring the cream mixture back to a boil over medium-high heat, and immediately pour it over the chocolate in the food processor. Wait 1 minute to let the chocolate melt completely, then pulse until the mixture is completely smooth. Add the butter and pulse until it is incorporated and the ganache is homogeneous and shiny.

Pour the ganache into a shallow pan, and let it cool at room temperature until it becomes pipeable, about 15 minutes, stirring occasionally. To check, periodically use a small spoon to scoop out some of the ganache. If it holds a ball-like shape, it is ready. This ganache can be kept covered and refrigerated for up to 1 week.

Variation: Chocolate-Tarragon

This ganache does not keep because its flavor changes over time; immediately use it to fill macarons, and eat them within 1 day.

Replace the mint with 3 packed tablespoons (11 grams) tarragon leaves, increase the light corn syrup to 3 tablespoons, and replace the milk chocolate with bittersweet chocolate.

Matcha is green tea powder, which you can *find in tea stores and online (see Resources, page 257). The deep green color is particularly pretty with Cocoa (page 75) or Almond (page 40) shells, and complementary to Green Tea Shells (page 86).*

Green Tea and White Chocolate

MAKES 1 PINT, ENOUGH FOR 40 SMALL SANDWICHED MACARONS

12 ounces (343 grams) white chocolate, chopped
½ teaspoon (1 gram) matcha powder
2 tablespoons (8 grams) loose green tea, or 4 tea bags
1 cup (240 grams) heavy cream

Put the chocolate in the bowl of a food processor and pulse several times until it is chopped into small pieces. Leave the chocolate in the processor and sprinkle the matcha powder over it.

Bring the tea and cream to a boil in a small saucepan over medium-high heat. Let it steep for 5 minutes, then press the tea to extract as much flavor as possible and strain it out from the cream. Bring the mixture back to a boil over medium-high heat. Immediately pour it over the chocolate in the food processor. Wait 1 minute to let the chocolate melt completely, then pulse until the mixture is completely smooth.

Pour the ganache into a shallow pan, and let it cool at room temperature until it becomes pipeable, about 30 minutes, stirring occasionally. To check, periodically use a small spoon to scoop out some of the ganache. If it holds a ball-like shape, it is ready. This ganache can be kept covered and refrigerated for up to 2 weeks.

This filling started out as a tart I created for one of my classes at the Institute of Culinary Education in New York. It makes for a stunning macaron when paired with Pink Peppercorn Shells (page 101). White chocolate can be overly sweet, so I like to combine it with ingredients that will cut through that sweetness and make for a well-balanced dessert. It also takes longer to set than darker chocolates.

White Chocolate— Grapefruit

MAKES 1 PINT, ENOUGH FOR
40 SMALL SANDWICHED MACARONS

14 ounces (400 grams) white chocolate, chopped

1 cup (240 grams) heavy cream

1½ packed teaspoons (6 grams) finely grated grapefruit zest (from 1 small grapefruit)

4 pink peppercorns

1 tablespoon (14 grams) unsalted butter, softened and cut into 4 pieces

¼ cup (60 grams) freshly squeezed and strained grapefruit juice (from 1 small grapefruit)

½ teaspoon (1.5 grams) vanilla extract

Put the chocolate in the bowl of a food processor and pulse several times until it is chopped into small pieces. Leave the chocolate in the processor.

Bring the cream, grapefruit zest, and peppercorns to a boil in a small saucepan over medium-high heat. Remove from the heat and let the mixture infuse for 10 minutes. Strain out the zest and peppercorns, then bring the mixture back to a boil over medium-high heat. Immediately pour it over the chocolate in the food processor. Wait 1 minute to let the chocolate melt completely, then pulse until the mixture is completely smooth. Add the butter and pulse until it is completely incorporated and the ganache is homogeneous and shiny, then, with the food processor running, add in the grapefruit juice and the vanilla extract.

Pour the ganache into a shallow pan, and let it cool at room temperature until it becomes pipeable, about 30 minutes, stirring occasionally. To check, periodically use a small spoon to scoop out some of the ganache. If it holds a ball-like shape, it is ready. This ganache can be kept covered and refrigerated for up to 1 week.

Lemon— Star Anise

Anne often adds a star anise and a slice of *lemon to a cup of black tea—the spicy and tart combination is heavenly. You can further accentuate the licorice taste of star anise by pairing this filling with Licorice Shells (page 79). Lemon Shells (page 78) are another option.*

MAKES 1 PINT, ENOUGH FOR
40 SMALL SANDWICHED MACARONS

11 ounces (320 grams) semisweet chocolate, chopped

1 cup (240 grams) heavy cream

2 tablespoons (36 grams) light corn syrup

1 packed tablespoon (12 grams) finely grated lemon zest (from 3 lemons)

3 whole star anise

1 tablespoon (14 grams) unsalted butter, softened and cut into 4 pieces

¼ cup plus 1 tablespoon (60 grams) freshly squeezed and strained lemon juice (from 2 lemons)

Put the chocolate in the bowl of a food processor and pulse several times until it is chopped into small pieces. Leave the chocolate in the processor.

Bring the cream, corn syrup, lemon zest, and star anise to a boil in a small saucepan over medium-high heat. Remove from the heat and let the mixture infuse for 10 minutes. Strain out the lemon zest and star anise, then bring the mixture back to a boil over medium-high heat. Immediately pour it over the chocolate in the food processor. Wait 1 minute to let the chocolate melt completely, then pulse until the mixture is completely smooth. Add the butter and pulse until it is completely incorporated and the ganache is homogeneous and shiny, then, with the food processor running, add in the lemon juice.

Pour the ganache into a shallow pan, and let it cool at room temperature until it becomes pipeable, about 15 minutes, stirring occasionally. To check, periodically use a small spoon to scoop out some of the ganache. If it holds a ball-like shape, it is ready. This ganache can be kept covered and refrigerated for up to 1 week.

Chai

Chai is a blend of black tea, cardamom, and

cinnamon from India. Different regions of the country also add black pepper, ginger, and cloves, as I found out when traveling throughout India and drinking chai anywhere I could find it. Most coffee shops on our side of the world offer chai lattes these days, which are often too sweet and a far cry from the original beverage. While this filling is sweet, too, the spices are its focus. Use it to fill Cardamom (page 84) or Cinnamon (page 84) shells.

MAKES 1 PINT, ENOUGH FOR
40 SMALL SANDWICHED MACARONS

(*continued*)

5½ ounces (160 grams) semisweet chocolate, chopped
5½ ounces (160 grams) milk chocolate, chopped
1 cup (240 grams) heavy cream
¼ cup (57 grams) milk
8 black peppercorns
6 cardamom pods
4 whole cloves
3 cinnamon sticks
2 tablespoons (8 grams) loose black tea, or 4 tea bags
2 tablespoons (36 grams) light corn syrup
1 tablespoon (14 grams) unsalted butter, softened and cut into 4 pieces

Pulse the chocolate in a food processor several times until it is chopped into small pieces.

Bring the cream, milk, peppercorns, cardamom, cloves, and cinnamon to a slow boil in a small saucepan over low heat. Remove from the heat, stir in the tea, and let the mixture infuse for 5 minutes.

Press the spices and tea to extract as much flavor as possible, then strain them out from the cream mixture. Add in the corn syrup and bring the mixture back to a boil over medium-high heat. Immediately pour it over the chocolate in the food processor. Wait 1 minute to let the chocolate melt completely, then pulse until the mixture is completely smooth. Add the butter and pulse until it is completely incorporated and the ganache is homogeneous and shiny.

Pour the ganache into a shallow pan, and let it cool at room temperature until it becomes pipeable, about 15 minutes, stirring occasionally. To check, periodically use a small spoon to scoop out some of the ganache. If it holds a ball-like shape, it is ready. This ganache can be kept covered and refrigerated for up to 2 weeks.

IMAGE ON LEFT: *Passion Fruit Shells with Chai Ganache*

Lapsang Souchong is a smoked tea from
China, with a very deep and unique flavor that the addition of whiskey nicely accentuates here. It evokes the wood-paneled walls of a library and deep, worn leather chairs, and is a great mignardise to serve at the end of a meal. Because the filling has such personality, I usually only pair it with Almond Shells (page 40).

Lapsang Souchong with Whiskey

MAKES 1 PINT, ENOUGH FOR 40 SMALL SANDWICHED MACARONS

11 ounces (320 grams) bittersweet chocolate pieces
2 tablespoons (8 grams) loose Lapsang Souchong, or 4 tea bags
1 cup (240 grams) heavy cream
2 tablespoons (36 grams) light corn syrup
1 tablespoon (14 grams) unsalted butter, softened and cut into 4 pieces
1 tablespoon (13 grams) whiskey

Put the chocolate in the bowl of a food processor and pulse several times until it is chopped into small pieces. Leave the chocolate in the processor.

Bring the tea, cream, and corn syrup to a boil in a small saucepan over medium-high heat. Let it steep for 5 minutes, then press the tea to extract as much flavor as possible and strain it out from the cream mixture. Bring the mixture back to a boil over medium-high heat. Immediately pour it over the chocolate in the food processor. Wait 1 minute to let the chocolate melt completely, then pulse until the mixture is completely smooth. Add the

butter and pulse until it is completely incorporated and the ganache is homogeneous and shiny, then, with the food processor running, add in the whiskey.

Pour the ganache into a shallow pan, and let it cool at room temperature until it becomes pipeable, about 15 minutes, stirring occasionally. To check, periodically use a small spoon to scoop out some of the ganache. If it holds a ball-like shape, it is ready. This ganache can be kept covered and refrigerated for up to 2 weeks.

Variation: Earl Grey

Earl Grey is a bergamot-flavored black tea. Its citrus notes make this filling a natural pairing for Orange Shells (page 77). Almond Shells (page 40) also work well.

Replace the tea with 2 tablespoons (8 grams) loose Earl Grey, or 4 tea bags. Replace the whiskey with 1 teaspoon (3 grams) of orange blossom water.

The bright purple color of this filling is

stunning and allows for really dramatic macarons when you pair it with similarly striking shells, such as Blackberry (page 81), Licorice (page 79), or the pure white of Almond Shells (page 40). You can buy black currant purée through specialty retailers and online (see Resource List, page 257). You can also substitute raspberry or blackberry purée made by blending frozen fruits that have been thawed, or use Blackberry Jelly (page 198). The jelly is a little sweeter than a purée, so if you use it, don't add corn syrup here. This ganache is best made a day ahead since it needs more time to set.

Cassis— White Chocolate

MAKES 1 PINT, ENOUGH FOR
40 SMALL SANDWICHED MACARONS

14 ounces (400 grams) white chocolate, chopped
¾ cup (180 grams) heavy cream
½ cup (120 grams) black currant purée (cassis), strained
2 tablespoons (36 grams) light corn syrup
1 tablespoon (14 grams) unsalted butter, softened
1 tablespoon (13 grams) crème de cassis

Put the chocolate in the bowl of a food processor and pulse several times until it is chopped into small pieces. Leave the chocolate in the processor.

Bring the cream, corn syrup, and black currant purée to a boil in a small saucepan over medium-high heat. Immediately pour it over the chocolate in the food processor. Wait 1 minute to let the chocolate melt completely, then

pulse until the mixture is completely smooth. Add the butter and pulse until it is completely incorporated and the ganache is homogeneous and shiny, then, with the food processor running, add in the crème de cassis.

Pour the ganache into a bowl or container, and let it cool until the bowl is no longer hot to the touch. Cover and refrigerate it for 12 to 24 hours before filling the macarons. It can be kept covered and refrigerated for up to 1 week.

MELTING CHOCOLATE

YOU CAN USE A DOUBLE-BOILER, WHICH WILL TAKE ABOUT FIVE minutes, or a microwave.

TO USE A DOUBLE BOILER: Bring a pan filled halfway with water to a boil over medium-high heat. Reduce the heat to low, and place the measured and chopped chocolate in a bowl that can fit over the pan without touching the water. Let the chocolate melt, stirring it just a few times with a rubber spatula and being careful not to let water splatter into the bowl and cause the chocolate to seize. It will take about 5 minutes, but pay close attention, particularly if melting a small amount of chocolate, so that it does not burn.

TO USE A MICROWAVE: Place the measured and chopped chocolate in a microwave-safe container. Heat it in 20-second increments, stirring between each, until it is melted.

Think of this filling as a homemade Nutella,

the beloved Italian hazelnut and chocolate breakfast spread. Praline paste is a purée of hazelnuts and caramelized sugar. You can buy it at gourmet grocery stores, specialty pastry retailers, or online (see Resources, page 257). Pair it with Hazelnut Shells (page 68).

Crunchy Hazelnut Gianduja

**MAKES 1 PINT, ENOUGH FOR
40 SMALL SANDWICHED MACARONS**

3 ounces (90 grams) milk chocolate, chopped
4 ounces (120 grams) semisweet chocolate, chopped
1 cup (240 grams) praline paste
Hazelnut Nougatine (recipe follows)
Pinch fine sea salt

Melt the milk and semisweet chocolates in a double boiler or in the microwave (see page 125 for specific instructions). Once the chocolate is melted, stir in the praline paste, hazelnut nougatine, and salt until the ganache is homogenous.

Pour the ganache into a shallow pan, and let it cool at room temperature until it becomes pipeable, about 20 minutes, stirring occasionally. To check, periodically use a small spoon to scoop out some of the ganache. If it holds a ball-like shape, it is ready. This ganache can be kept covered and refrigerated for up to 1 month.

Hazelnut Nougatine

1 cup (200 grams) granulated sugar
¾ cup (120 grams) hazelnuts, blanched and toasted (see page 135)

Line a baking sheet with parchment paper.

Cook the sugar in a small saucepan over medium heat until it turns a clear amber color, the edges begin to foam, and you can smell the caramel, about 5 minutes. Stir only if the sugar does not melt evenly. Remove from the heat and quickly stir in the hazelnuts. Pour the caramel into the baking sheet and let it cool completely, until it is hard, about 20 minutes.

Transfer the caramel to the bowl of a food processor, and process until it is broken into even-sized crunchy bits, about 8 pulses. The crunch can stored in an airtight container at room temperature for up to 1 month.

Variation: Peanut Gianduja
Use this filling with Blackberry Jelly (page 198), for a fun twist on peanut butter and jelly sandwiches. Pair it with Strawberry Shells (page 82).

Substitute 1 cup (240 grams) crunchy or smooth peanut butter for the praline paste and nougatine and add 1 teaspoon (3 grams) vanilla extract.

CREAMY FILLINGS

VANILLA BUTTERCREAM ✶ MAPLE BUTTERCREAM ✶

PISTACHIO BUTTERCREAM ✶ BASIL BUTTERCREAM

✶ SESAME BUTTERCREAM ✶ OATMEAL COOKIE

BUTTERCREAM ✶ PUMPKIN-BOURBON BUTTERCREAM ✶

Variation: Gingerbread Buttercream ✶

ORANGE CREAM ✶ GINGER CREAM ✶

PEAR CREAM ✶ LEMON CURD ✶ KEY LIME CURD ✶

POPCORN PASTRY CREAM ✶ PASSION FRUIT

PASTRY CREAM ✶ CHERRY-ALMOND CREAM ✶

✶ LEMON-ALMOND CREAM

These fillings represent many of the ways in which you can obtain creaminess in pastry—most often, without actually using any actual cream. It's all about texture, and air beaten into other ingredients to make them fluffy. Buttercream is a type of icing often used on cakes. It is either meringue-based (as it is here, where an Italian-style meringue is formed with heated sugar syrup) or confectioners' sugar-based (an American style of buttercream). Meringue-based buttercreams can be flavored in infinite ways to fill macarons, and freeze well. Most of the recipes here will keep for up to two weeks in the refrigerator, and one month in the freezer.

A curd is a thick, creamy custard that is made by stirring the ingredients over a heat source. Typically, a citrus juice is cooked with eggs and sugar. Pastry cream is also a stirred custard, with a consistency similar to pudding. The milk it contains can be flavored with a wide range of ingredients through an infusion process.

In France, macarons are often simply filled with almond paste that is beaten with butter and then flavored many different ways. Two options are offered here, but feel free to experiment with others, especially if you have other fillings leftover that could be folded into an almond cream.

Buttercream will freeze well for up to a month. Let it thaw in the refrigerator and bring it to room temperature 2 hours before assembling the macarons.

IF YOU DO NOT OWN A CANDY THERMOMETER, check the temperature of the sugar syrup by dropping a few drops of syrup into ice water (use a heatproof spoon or spatula to do so). The syrup should feel a bit sticky and form a soft ball in the water. Visually, once it reaches 238°F (115°C), the syrup will be bubbling (large and small bubbles) throughout the entire surface of the pan, and will remain translucent.

CHEFS COOK THE SYRUP USED IN BUTTERCREAMS with a wide range of temperatures, depending on the size of the batch they are making and how long they want to keep the product. Because these fillings are small, the syrup will continue to cook in the pan as you pour it into the egg whites when making buttercream. Bringing it to 238°F (115°C) on a thermometer may prevent overcooking it, which can happen quickly.

PIPING BUTTERCREAM

SPOON THE BUTTERCREAM INTO A PASTRY BAG AND CUT A ½-INCH opening at the tip (or use a ½-inch tip). Pipe a small amount of buttercream, about ½-inch thick, in a circular shape, on the flat sides of the shells. Don't let the buttercream go all the way to the edges of the macaron. Top with another shell, twisting it slightly to secure the filling.

Vanilla buttercream is one of the most basic *and versatile macaron fillings you can make, since it will go with nearly every shell flavor. The seeds of the vanilla bean give a speckled appearance, but because the taste can be mild, I like to add vanilla extract as well, for a full vanilla effect.*

MAKES 1 PINT, ENOUGH FOR
40 SMALL SANDWICHED MACARONS

1 vanilla bean

1 cup (200 grams) granulated sugar

3 egg whites

Pinch cream of tartar

¼ teaspoon (1 gram) fine sea salt

2 sticks (227 grams) cold unsalted butter,
  cut into 1-inch cubes

1 tablespoon (9 grams) vanilla extract

Vanilla Buttercream

Split the vanilla bean in half lengthwise, and use the back of a paring knife to scrape out the seeds. Stir them into the granulated sugar, and rub the bean into the sugar to extract as many seeds as possible.

Put the egg whites and cream of tartar in the bowl of an electric mixer fitted with the whisk attachment.

Bring the sugar and ¼ cup (57 grams) water to a boil in a small saucepan over medium-high heat, stirring to dissolve the sugar. Clip a candy

(*continued*)

thermometer to the pan and cook until the mixture reaches 238°F (115°C).

While the syrup is cooking, whisk the egg whites at medium speed until they form soft peaks, about 2 minutes. Once the syrup reaches 238°F (115°C), quickly remove the vanilla bean with kitchen tongs, then gradually and steadily pour the syrup down the side of the bowl, resting the edge of the pan on the edge of the mixer so that the syrup does not hit the whisk attachment and splatter. This process should take 15 seconds. Whisk the meringue until stiff peaks form and the bowl cools down, about 8 minutes.

Add the salt and butter and whisk on high speed until the meringue emulsifies and becomes completely smooth and fluffy, about 8 minutes. Add the vanilla extract. This buttercream can be kept covered and refrigerated for up to 2 weeks.

YOU MIGHT NEED TO LIFT THE BOWL SLIGHTLY with your hands while whipping the egg whites at the beginning of the process, in case the amount is too small for the whisk to reach them. Once they start gaining volume, you can leave it in its normal position.

This buttercream uses maple syrup instead *of sugar to form the meringue. Pair it with Walnut, Pecan, or Hazelnut (page 68) shells to accentuate the fall-winter feel of the filling.*

Maple Buttercream

MAKES 1 PINT, ENOUGH FOR
40 SMALL SANDWICHED MACARONS

3 egg whites
Pinch cream of tartar
1¼ cups (425 grams) maple syrup
¼ teaspoon (1 gram) fine sea salt
2 sticks (227 grams) cold unsalted butter,
    cut into 1-inch cubes

Put the egg whites and cream of tartar in the bowl of an electric mixer fitted with the whisk attachment.

Bring the maple syrup to a boil in a small saucepan over medium-high heat. Clip a thermometer to the pan and cook until the mixture reaches 238°F (115°C).

While the maple syrup is cooking, whisk the egg whites at medium speed until they form soft peaks, about 2 minutes. Once the maple syrup reaches 238°F (115°C), gradually and steadily pour it down the side of the bowl, resting the edge of the pan on the mixer so that the syrup does not hit the whisk attachment and splatter. This process should take 15 seconds. Whisk the meringue until stiff peaks form and the bowl cools down, about 8 minutes.

Add the salt and butter and whisk on high speed until the meringue emulsifies and becomes completely smooth and fluffy, about 8 minutes. This buttercream can be kept covered and refrigerated for up to 2 weeks.

This versatile filling works wonders with a range of shell flavors, including Pistachio (page 68), Cocoa (page 75), any of the fruit-flavored shells, and Almond Shells (page 40). Many pastry shops add green food coloring and almond extract to pistachio products to make them taste more "pistachio-ey," which often results in an artificial taste. None of that here: toasting the nuts and grinding them with syrup give them a more pronounced flavor naturally.

Pistachio Buttercream

MAKES 1 PINT, ENOUGH FOR 40 SMALL SANDWICHED MACARONS

¾ cup (83 grams) shelled pistachios, preferably Sicilian, toasted (see page 135)

1¼ cups (250 grams) granulated sugar, divided

¼ teaspoon (1 gram) fine sea salt

3 egg whites

Pinch cream of tartar

2 sticks (227 grams) cold unsalted butter, cut into 1-inch cubes

Preheat the oven to 350°F (175°C). Place the pistachios in the bowl of a food processor.

Bring ½ cup (100 grams) sugar, the salt, and ⅛ cup (28.5 grams) water to a boil in a small saucepan over medium-high heat. Clip a candy thermometer to the pan, reduce the heat to medium, and cook until the mixture reaches 230°F (110°C). Pour the syrup over the pistachios and process until the mixture forms the smoothest purée possible. Set aside while you proceed.

Put the egg whites and cream of tartar in the bowl of an electric mixer fitted with the whisk attachment.

Bring the remaining ¾ cup (150 grams) sugar and ¼ cup (57 grams) water to a boil in a small saucepan over medium-high heat, stirring to dissolve the sugar. Clip a candy thermometer to the pan and cook until the mixture reaches 238°F (115°C).

While the syrup is cooking, whisk the egg whites at medium speed until they form soft peaks, about 2 minutes. Once the syrup reaches 238°F (115°C), gradually and steadily pour the syrup down the side of the bowl, resting the edge of the pan on the edge of the mixer so that the syrup does not hit the whisk attachment and splatter. This process should take 15 seconds. Whisk the meringue until stiff peaks form and the bowl cools down, about 8 minutes.

Add the butter and whisk on high speed until the meringue emulsifies and becomes completely smooth and fluffy, about 8 minutes. Add in the pistachio purée while the mixer is running and whisk until the buttercream returns to a smooth and fluffy state. It can be kept covered and refrigerated for up to 2 weeks.

TOASTING NUTS

PREHEAT THE OVEN TO 350°F (175°C).

Spread the nuts on a baking sheet and bake them in the oven until they are toasted through, about 6 minutes. To check that the nuts are ready, break one open and taste it. The oil content varies depending on the type of nut, so if you start to smell them earlier, open one up to check—they might be ready.

I have a large herb and flower garden, so am *always looking for ways to use its products in my baking. In the middle of summer, after weeks of using basil in all its possible savory applications, I am usually ready for more unusual ways to dispense of my plants' abundant crop. This buttercream tastes of basil, there is no question about that, but it is not a savory filling per se; rather, it is a sweet buttercream with herbal notes. Pair it with Pink Peppercorn (page 101), Strawberry (page 82), or, for a complete garden experience, Marigold (page 88) shells.*

Basil Buttercream

MAKES 1 PINT, ENOUGH FOR 40 SMALL SANDWICHED MACARONS

1 large bunch (50 grams) basil
1 cup (200 grams) granulated sugar
3 egg whites
Pinch cream of tartar
¼ teaspoon (1 gram) fine sea salt
2 sticks (227 grams) cold unsalted butter, cut into 1-inch cubes

Remove the basil leaves from their stalks and wash them. Bring them to a boil with ¾ cup (172 grams) water in a small saucepan on medium-high heat. Remove from the heat, stir in the sugar, and let the leaves infuse for 20 minutes.

(*continued*)

IMAGE ON RIGHT: *Cocoa Shells with Basil Buttercream*

When the mixture is cool, transfer it to a blender and blend for 2 minutes, pulsing rather than letting it run constantly.

Put the egg whites and cream of tartar in the bowl of an electric mixer fitted with the whisk attachment. Bring the basil-sugar mixture to a boil in a small saucepan over medium-high heat. Clip a candy thermometer to the pan and cook until the mixture reaches 238°F (115°C).

While the syrup is cooking, whisk the egg whites at medium speed until they form soft peaks, about 2 minutes. Once the syrup reaches 238°F (115°C), gradually and steadily pour the syrup down the side of the bowl, resting the edge of the pan on the edge of the mixer so that the syrup does not hit the whisk attachment and splatter. This process should take 15 seconds. Whisk the meringue until stiff peaks form and the bowl cools down, about 8 minutes.

Add the salt and butter and whisk on high speed until the meringue emulsifies and becomes completely smooth and fluffy, about 8 minutes. This buttercream can be kept covered and refrigerated for up to 2 weeks.

Sesame brittle is a snack often found in

Middle Eastern or health food stores. It is easy to make by hand, and will add texture as well as flavor to this sesame buttercream. It's a nice change from peanut or almond brittle, and makes a great filling for Sesame (page 102) or Lime (page 78) shells.

Sesame Buttercream

MAKES 1 PINT, ENOUGH FOR
40 SMALL SANDWICHED MACARONS

3 egg whites
Pinch cream of tartar
1 cup (200 grams) granulated sugar
2 sticks (227 grams) cold unsalted butter,
   cut into 1-inch cubes
1 teaspoon (3 grams) vanilla extract
2 drops sesame oil
Sesame Brittle (recipe follows)

Put the egg whites and cream of tartar in the bowl of an electric mixer fitted with the whisk attachment.

Bring the sugar and ¼ cup (57 grams) water to a boil in a small saucepan over medium-high heat, stirring to dissolve the sugar. Clip a candy thermometer to the pan and cook until the mixture reaches 238°F (115°C).

While the syrup is cooking, whisk the egg whites at medium speed until they form soft peaks, about 2 minutes. Once the syrup reaches 238°F

(continued)

(115°C), gradually and steadily pour the syrup down the side of the bowl, resting the edge of the pan on the edge of the mixer so that the syrup does not hit the whisk attachment and splatter. This process should take 15 seconds. Whisk the meringue until stiff peaks form and the bowl cools down, about 8 minutes.

Add the butter and whisk on high speed until the meringue emulsifies and becomes completely smooth and fluffy, about 8 minutes. Add the vanilla extract and sesame oil while the mixer is running and whisk until the buttercream returns to a smooth and fluffy state. Remove from the mixer and stir in the powdered brittle. This buttercream can be kept covered and refrigerated for up to 2 weeks.

Sesame Brittle

MAKES ½ CUP

¾ cup (150 grams) granulated sugar
½ cup (70 grams) white sesame seeds, toasted (see page 135)
¼ teaspoon (1 gram) fleur de sel

Line a baking sheet with parchment paper.

Cook the sugar in a small saucepan over medium-high heat until it turns a clear amber color, the edges begin to foam, and you can smell the caramel, about 5 minutes. Stir only if the sugar does not melt evenly. Remove from the heat and quickly stir in the sesame seeds and fleur de sel. Pour the caramel into the baking sheet and let it cool for 15 minutes.

Transfer the brittle to the bowl of a food processor, and process until it turns into a medium-fine powder, about 8 pulses. The brittle can be made up to 3 days ahead and stored at room temperature in an airtight container.

This filling takes oatmeal from breakfast

to a special treat, just like the cookies that inspired it. Don't use the amount of water specified on the oatmeal container—the filling would be too liquid. It needs to be thick enough to be pipeable. Also note the shorter storage life. Pair it with Orange (page 77) or Walnut (page 68) shells.

Oatmeal Cookie Buttercream

MAKES 1 PINT, ENOUGH FOR
40 SMALL SANDWICHED MACARONS

¼ cup (32 grams) instant oatmeal,
   plain with no added sugar

⅓ cup (76 grams) boiling water

½ cup (50 grams) raisins, finely diced

¼ teaspoon (.5 grams) ground cinnamon

3 egg whites

Pinch cream of tartar

1 cup (200 grams) granulated sugar

¼ teaspoon (1 gram) fine sea salt

2½ sticks (283 grams) cold unsalted butter,
   cut into 1-inch cubes

1 tablespoon (9 grams) vanilla extract

Combine the instant oatmeal and the boiling water. Add the raisins and cinnamon to the oatmeal, stir, and set aside. It will be thick.

Put the egg whites and cream of tartar in the bowl of an electric mixer fitted with the whisk attachment.

(continued)

Bring the sugar and $\frac{1}{4}$ cup (57 grams) water to a boil in a small saucepan over medium-high heat, stirring to dissolve the sugar. Clip a candy thermometer to the pan and cook until the mixture reaches 238°F (115°C).

While the syrup is cooking, whisk the egg whites at medium speed until they form soft peaks. Once the syrup reaches 238°F (115°C), gradually and steadily pour the syrup down the side of the bowl, resting the edge of the pan on the edge of the mixer so that the syrup does not hit the whisk attachment and splatter. This process should take 15 seconds. Whisk the meringue until stiff peaks form and the bowl cools down, about 8 minutes.

Add the salt and butter and whisk on high speed until the meringue emulsifies and becomes completely smooth and fluffy, about 8 minutes. Add the vanilla extract and oatmeal-raising mixture while the mixer is running and whisk until the buttercream returns to a smooth and fluffy state. It can be kept covered and refrigerated for up to 3 days.

Here is another seasonal filling, which I like to serve throughout the fall, but most particularly at Thanksgiving. With Pecan (page 68), Five-Spice (page 85), or Ginger (page 85) shells, these macarons are a great alternative to pie at the end of a substantial meal. This filling also has a shorter storage time, because of the barely cooked pumpkin.

MAKES 1 PINT, ENOUGH FOR
40 SMALL SANDWICHED MACARONS

Pumpkin-Bourbon Buttercream

3 egg whites

Pinch cream of tartar

1 cup (200 grams) granulated sugar

¼ teaspoon (1 gram) fine sea salt

2½ sticks (283 grams) cold unsalted butter, cut into 1-inch cubes

1 tablespoon (13 grams) bourbon

1 cup (236 grams) canned pumpkin purée

1 teaspoon (2.75 grams) ground cinnamon

1 teaspoon (2 grams) ground ginger

½ teaspoon (1 gram) freshly grated nutmeg

¼ teaspoon (.5 gram) ground cloves

Put the egg whites and cream of tartar in the bowl of an electric mixer fitted with the whisk attachment.

(continued)

Bring the sugar and $^1/_4$ cup (57 grams) water to a boil in a small saucepan over medium-high heat, stirring to dissolve the sugar. Clip a candy thermometer to the pan and cook until the mixture reaches 238°F (115°C).

While the syrup is cooking, whisk the egg whites at medium speed until they form soft peaks, about 2 minutes. Once the syrup reaches 238°F (115°C), gradually and steadily pour the syrup down the side of the bowl, resting the edge of the pan on the edge of the mixer so that the syrup does not hit the whisk attachment and splatter. This process should take 15 seconds. Whisk the meringue until stiff peaks form and the bowl cools down, about 8 minutes.

Add the salt and butter and whisk on high speed until the meringue emulsifies and becomes completely smooth and fluffy, about 8 minutes. Add the bourbon, pumpkin purée, cinnamon, ginger, nutmeg, and cloves while the mixer is running and whisk until the buttercream returns to a smooth and fluffy state. It can be kept covered and refrigerated for up to 3 days.

Variation: Gingerbread Buttercream

This makes an ideal holiday macaron. Use it to fill Five-Spice Shells (page 85), pack them in beautiful boxes, and bring them as gifts to the parties you'll be attending throughout the holidays. The yield is smaller: $1^1/_2$ cups.

Omit the pumpkin and bourbon. Reduce the butter to 2 sticks (227 grams). Add the spices at the same time you do the butter and salt. Once all the butter is incorporated, add 1 teaspoon (3 grams) of vanilla extract and 2 tablespoons (32 grams) of crystallized ginger, finely chopped, while the mixer is running and whisk until the buttercream returns to a smooth and fluffy state.

This cream and the two that follow were *inspired by famed French pastry chef Pierre Hermé's lemon curd, in which the butter does not melt, making for a light, mousse-like filling. Adding lemon juice to the orange juice gives this cream a more intense flavor. It pairs well with Marigold (page 88) and Orange (page 77) shells, as well as with any of the nut ones. Because it is quite rich, you don't need as much to fill the macarons.*

Orange Cream

MAKES 1 PINT, ENOUGH FOR
40 SMALL SANDWICHED MACARONS

1 egg

5 egg yolks

¾ cup plus 2 tablespoons (180 grams) granulated sugar

¾ cup (144 grams) freshly squeezed and strained
orange juice (from 3 oranges)

2 tablespoons (24 grams) freshly squeezed and strained lemon
juice (from 1 lemon)

1 packed tablespoon (12 grams) finely grated orange zest
(from 2 oranges)

1 packed teaspoon (4 grams) finely grated lemon zest
(from 1 lemon)

Pinch fine sea salt

2 sticks (227 grams) unsalted butter, softened

Bring the eggs, yolks, sugar, orange juice, lemon juice, orange zest, lemon zest, and sea salt to a boil in a medium non-reactive stainless steel saucepan *(continued)*

over medium heat, whisking constantly, about 8 minutes. Once it boils, whisk vigorously for 1 minute over the heat.

Remove from the heat and strain through a fine-mesh strainer. Let the mixture cool until it is lukewarm.

Pour the mixture into a blender, add the butter, and process the mixture until it is smooth and emulsified, about 1 minute. Pour it into a container and let it cool to room temperature, then cover and refrigerate it overnight, until it reaches a mousse-like consistency. This cream can be kept covered and refrigerated for up to 4 days.

I can never have enough ginger, and am always *looking for new desserts in which to include it. I used to make this cream to fill petits fours when working at Windows on the World, and then decided to pair it with Ginger Shells (page 85) when I started baking macarons. It also works well with any of the nut shells.*

Ginger Cream

MAKES 1½ CUPS, ENOUGH FOR 40 SMALL SANDWICHED MACARONS

2 eggs

3 egg yolks

1½ cups (300 grams) granulated sugar

2 packed tablespoons (60 grams) peeled and finely grated fresh ginger (6-inch piece)

1½ packed teaspoons (6 grams) finely grated
    orange zest (from 1 orange)

1 teaspoon (3 grams) vanilla extract

Pinch fine sea salt

1½ sticks (170 grams) unsalted butter, softened

Bring the eggs, yolks, sugar, grated ginger, orange zest, vanilla extract, and sea salt to a boil in a medium non-reactive stainless steel saucepan over medium heat, whisking constantly, about 8 minutes. Once it boils, whisk vigorously for 1 minute over the heat.

Remove from the heat and strain through a fine-mesh strainer. Let the mixture cool until it is lukewarm.

Pour the mixture into a blender, add the butter, and process the mixture until it is smooth and emulsified, about 1 minute. Pour it into a container and let it cool to room temperature, then cover and refrigerate it overnight, until it reaches a mousse-like consistency. This cream can be kept covered and refrigerated for up to 4 days.

Pear Cream

This unusual filling is a perfect fall treat *when used to fill Hazelnut (page 68), Cocoa (page 75), Vanilla (page 72), or Almond (page 34) shells. You can substitute canned pears; just make sure to drain them well. Poire Williams is a pear-based eau-de-vie.*

MAKES 1 PINT, ENOUGH FOR
40 SMALL SANDWICHED MACARONS

6 very ripe medium pears, peeled and cored

2 teaspoons (8 grams) freshly squeezed and strained lemon juice (from ½ lemon)

4 eggs

4 egg yolks

2 cups (400 grams) granulated sugar

1 tablespoon (13 grams) Poire Williams

1½ sticks (170 grams) unsalted butter, softened

Put the pears and lemon juice in a food processor and purée until smooth.

Bring the eggs, yolks, sugar, and pear purée to a boil in a medium saucepan over medium heat, whisking constantly, about 8 minutes. Once it boils, whisk vigorously for 1 minute over the heat.

Remove from the heat, stir in the Poire Williams, and strain through a fine-mesh strainer. Let the mixture cool until it is lukewarm, then pour it into a blender, add the butter, and process the mixture until it is smooth and emulsified, about 1 minute. Pour it into a container and let it cool to room temperature, then cover and refrigerate it overnight, until it reaches a mousse-like consistency. This cream can be kept covered and refrigerated for up to 4 days.

Just like adding lemon juice to an orange-
based preparation boosts its flavor, so does a little bit of lime in a lemon
dessert. Here the lime zest also adds beautiful green speckles to the filling.
Pair it with Lemon-Poppy Seed (page 78), Marigold (page 88), Wasabi
(page 103), or Lime (page 78) shells.

MAKES 1 PINT, ENOUGH FOR
40 SMALL SANDWICHED MACARONS

1½ cups (288 grams) freshly squeezed
  and strained lemon juice (from 10 lemons)

2 packed teaspoons (8 grams) finely grated
  lemon zest (from 1 lemon)

1 packed teaspoon (4 grams) finely grated lime zest
  (from 1 lime)

4 eggs

5 egg yolks

1¼ cups (250 grams) granulated sugar

1 stick (114 grams) unsalted butter,
  softened and cut into tablespoons

Lemon Curd

Whisk together the lemon juice, lemon zest, lime zest, eggs, egg yolks, and
sugar in a medium non-reactive stainless steel saucepan until they reach a
homogenized mixture. Cook over medium heat, whisking constantly, until
the mixture comes to a boil, about 8 minutes. Once it boils, whisk vigorously
for 1 minute over the heat.

(continued)

Remove the curd from the heat and strain it into a medium-sized bowl. This will remove any piece of cooked eggs and ensure that the curd is smooth. Whisk in the butter until it is completely incorporated. Pour the curd into a shallow pan so that it can cool faster, and refrigerate it for at least 2 hours, until set. This curd can be kept covered and refrigerated for up to 4 days.

CURDS AND COOKED CREAM FILLINGS take longer to set than other types of creamy filling. Ideally, they should sit in the refrigerator for 12 hours before piping.

If you cannot find key limes, substitute regular ones, or even bottled key lime juice—but only the best quality brand you can find. Pair this filling with Cinnamon (page 84), Lime (page 78), Vanilla (page 72), or Almond (page 40) shells. It is also used in combination with a marshmallow filling to make Key Lime Macarons (page 212).

Key Lime Curd

MAKES 1 PINT, ENOUGH FOR
40 SMALL SANDWICHED MACARONS

2 cups (360 grams) freshly squeezed and strained
    key lime juice (from about 16 key limes)

1 packed teaspoon (4 grams) finely grated lime
    zest (from 1 lime)

4 eggs

5 egg yolks

1¼ cups (250 grams) granulated sugar

¼ teaspoon (.5 grams) fine sea salt

1 stick (114 grams) unsalted butter, softened
  and cut into tablespoons

Whisk together the lime juice, lime zest, eggs, egg yolks, sugar, and sea salt in a medium non-reactive stainless steel saucepan until they reach a homogenized mixture. Cook over medium heat, whisking constantly, until the mixture comes to a boil, about 8 minutes. Once it boils, whisk vigorously for 1 minute over the heat.

Remove the curd from the heat and strain it into a medium-sized bowl. This will remove any pieces of cooked eggs and ensure that the curd is smooth. Whisk in the butter until it is completely incorporated. Pour the curd into a shallow pan so that it can cool faster, and refrigerate it for at least 2 hours, until set. This curd can be kept covered and refrigerated for up to 4 days.

This pastry cream truly tastes like popcorn—the good, buttery kind—and is one of my favorite fillings in this book. I could eat it with a spoon, and will bake macarons simply to have an excuse to make it. If you like buttered popcorn Jelly Beans, you will love it too. It pairs well with Ancho Chile Shells (page 102) for a more savory flavor, or with Blackberry (page 81), Licorice (page 79), or Pecan (page 68) shells.

Popcorn Pastry Cream

MAKES 1 PINT, ENOUGH FOR
40 SMALL SANDWICHED MACARONS

¼ cup (50 grams) popcorn kernels

2 tablespoons (26 grams) extra-virgin olive oil

½ teaspoon (2 grams) fine sea salt

2½ cups (570 grams) whole milk, plus more if needed

¼ cup (32 grams) cornstarch

2 eggs

2 egg yolks

⅔ cup (134 grams) granulated sugar

3 tablespoons (42 grams) unsalted butter, softened

1 teaspoon (3 grams) vanilla extract

Heat the popcorn kernels and the olive oil over medium-high heat in a large stockpot covered with a lid. Once you hear the first kernels pop, after about
(continued)

IMAGE ON LEFT: *Blackberry Shells with Popcorn Pastry Cream*

4 minutes, start shaking the pot periodically, to ensure that no kernel sticks to the bottom of the pot and burns. Once all the kernels have popped, remove the popcorn from the heat and sprinkle the salt over it. Discard any unopened kernels.

Bring the milk to a boil in a medium saucepan over medium-high heat. Pour it over the popcorn and let the mixture infuse for 1 hour, stirring occasionally. Transfer the mixture to a blender and blend for 2 minutes, until smooth. Strain the mixture through a fine-mesh sieve to ensure that it is completely smooth.

In a medium bowl, whisk the cornstarch with the egg and egg yolks to dissolve it. Add a splash of the popcorn milk if necessary.

Bring the popcorn milk and sugar to a boil in a medium saucepan over medium heat, whisking frequently. Once the mixture is boiling, whisk in the cornstarch-egg mixture. Let it return to a boil until it is very thick and smooth, whisking constantly with vigor. Continue whisking for one minute.

Pour the mixture into the bowl of an electric mixer fitted with the whisk attachment. Add the butter and vanilla extract and whisk on medium-high speed until the mixture cools, about 15 minutes. It can be kept covered and refrigerated for up to 2 days. When the shells are filled, consume within 1 day.

You will find passion fruit purée in the
*freezer section of some gourmet and Latin American grocery stores, as well
as online (see Resources, page 257). Pair this filling with Passion Fruit (page
83), Coconut (page 68), or Green Tea (page 86) shells.*

Passion Fruit Pastry Cream

MAKES 1 PINT, ENOUGH FOR
40 SMALL SANDWICHED MACARONS

¼ cup (32 grams) cornstarch

2 eggs

2 egg yolks

¾ cup (180 grams) passion fruit purée

1¼ cups (300 grams) heavy cream

⅔ cup (134 grams) granulated sugar

3 tablespoons (42 grams) unsalted butter, softened

2 teaspoons (6 grams) vanilla extract

In a medium bowl, whisk the cornstarch with the egg and egg yolks to dissolve it. Add a splash of the passion fruit purée if necessary.

Bring the heavy cream, passion fruit purée, and sugar to a boil in a medium
saucepan over medium heat, whisking frequently. Once the mixture is boiling, whisk in the cornstarch-egg mixture. Let it boil for 1 minute, until it is very
thick and smooth, whisking constantly with vigor.

Pour the mixture into the bowl of an electric mixer fitted with the whisk
attachment. Add the butter and vanilla extract and whisk on medium-high
speed until it cools, about 15 minutes. It can be kept covered and refrigerated
for up to 2 days. When the shells are filled, consume within 1 day.

Maraschino is an Italian cherry liqueur *that is rather sweet, thick, and dark red. You can also substitute Kirsch, a colorless, cherry-flavored eau-de-vie. With a red filling, I like to use Vanilla (page 72), for color contrast. For Valentine's Day, you could pair it with pink shells such as Strawberry (page 82) or Rose (page 91) shells. This is a great recipe if you have Sour Cherry Compote (page 189) leftover after filling macaron shells.*

Cherry-Almond Cream

MAKES 1½ CUPS, ENOUGH FOR
40 SMALL SANDWICHED MACARONS

4 ounces (½ cup or 120 grams) almond paste
1 stick (114 grams) unsalted butter, cut into
   tablespoons, at room temperature
½ recipe Sour Cherry Compote (page 189)
2 tablespoons (26 grams) maraschino liqueur
Pinch fine sea salt

In the bowl of an electric mixer fitted with the paddle attachment, beat the almond paste on low speed to break it up. Slowly incorporate the butter while the mixer is running. When the butter is completely incorporated and the mixture is smooth, beat in the compote, maraschino, and salt. This cream can be kept covered and refrigerated for up to 2 weeks.

This almond paste-based cream has a coarser *texture than lemon curd would have on its own. It is relatively easy to prepare; I like to use it when I want to serve multiple fillings, and have already made lemon curd. Pair it with Almond (page 40), Cardamom (page 84), Violet (page 92), or Vanilla (page 72) shells.*

Lemon-Almond Cream

MAKES 1½ CUPS, ENOUGH FOR
40 SMALL SANDWICHED MACARONS

4 ounces (½ cup or 120 grams) almond paste
½ recipe Lemon Curd (page 149)
1 teaspoon (3 grams) vanilla extract
Pinch fine sea salt

In the bowl of an electric mixer fitted with the paddle attachment, beat the almond paste on low speed to break it up. Slowly pour in the lemon curd while the mixer is running. When the curd is completely incorporated and the mixture is smooth, add in the vanilla extract and salt. This cream can be kept covered and refrigerated for up to 4 days.

CARAMEL FILLINGS

FLEUR DE SEL CARAMEL ★ ROSEMARY CARAMEL ★

BLOOD ORANGE CARAMEL ★ COCONUT CARAMEL

★ RASPBERRY-WHITE CHOCOLATE CARAMEL

★ APRICOT-GINGER-CHOCOLATE CARAMEL ★

CREAMY DARK CHOCOLATE CARAMEL ★

Making caramel means cooking sugar syrup past the hard crack stage, when the sugars begin to take on complex flavors other than sweetness. Be careful when making caramel: You need to stop the cooking process either by adding a liquid to dilute the caramel, or pouring it out of the pan, which can result in splatters. The caramel at that point has a temperature of about 330°F (165°C), which will burn you severely if any reaches your bare arms or hands. Also resist the temptation to dip your finger in hot, luscious caramel— you will pay a high price for gourmandise.

Always use a heat-resistant utensil when working with caramel, so that it does not melt in the pan. Silicone spatulas and wooden or metal spoons all work.

PIPING CARAMEL

SPOON THE CARAMEL INTO A PASTRY BAG AND CUT A ¼-INCH OPEN-ing at the tip. Pipe a small amount of caramel, about ¼-inch thick, on the flat sides of the shells. Don't let the caramel go all the way to the edges of the macaron. Top with another shell, twist it slightly to secure the filling, and let set in the refrigerator, about 10 minutes.

These caramels are very rich; they also cause shells to slide if you fill them too much. For this reason, the yield of these recipes is slightly smaller. Evenly divide them among 40 shells.

Salty caramel has become ubiquitous in *pastry shops and restaurants around the country. It makes a great filling for Espresso (page 76) or Vanilla (page 72) shells, and, in a more special combination, Pink Peppercorn (page 101). For a more pronounced fleur de sel effect, sprinkle the salt over the filling before topping it with the second shell.*

Fleur de Sel Caramel

MAKES 1½ CUPS, ENOUGH FOR
40 SMALL SANDWICHED MACARONS

½ cup (120 grams) heavy cream

2 cups (400 grams) granulated sugar

1 teaspoon (4 grams) freshly squeezed and strained
    lemon juice (from ½ lemon)

⅛ teaspoon (.5 gram) fleur de sel

Heat the cream in a small saucepan over medium heat until it is scalding (almost to a boil), about 3 minutes.

Heat the sugar and lemon juice in a medium saucepan over medium heat. Stir with a wooden spoon or a heat-resistant spatula to "rub" the juice into the sugar until the sugar resembles wet sand. Cook until the sugar syrup turns a clear amber color, the edges begin to foam, and you can smell the caramel, about 10 minutes. Stir only if the sugar does not melt evenly.

Remove from the heat and immediately pour in the cream to stop the cooking process. Keep the pan away from you to avoid splatters. Whisk in

(continued)

IMAGE ON RIGHT: *Espresso Shells with Fleur de Sel Caramel*

the fleur de sel, pour the caramel into a container, and let it cool at room temperature for 2 hours. Cover, then refrigerate for 12 to 24 hours. It can be kept covered and refrigerated for up to 1 month.

IT IS BEST TO MAKE THESE FILLINGS 12 to 24 hours before piping them onto the shells, other than where indicated. This allows them to cool naturally and results in a better piping texture.

I started infusing herbs into sugar syrups

when I worked as a pastry chef in restaurants, and used those to add flavors to cakes or make sorbets and granitas. Rosemary adds earthiness to caramel, as well as a surprising flavor. I like it paired with Cocoa Shells (page 75), which tames it a little bit, but you can also keep with the unexpected theme and use Black Peppercorn (page 101) or Pecan (page 68) shells.

Rosemary Caramel

MAKES 1½ CUPS, ENOUGH FOR
40 SANDWICHED SMALL MACARONS

2 cups (400 grams) granulated sugar
2 tablespoon (36 grams) light corn syrup
½ cup (120 grams) heavy cream
1 small sprig rosemary
1 vanilla bean
Pinch of freshly ground black pepper

Heat the cream, rosemary, and vanilla bean in a small saucepan over medium heat until it is scalding (almost to a boil), about 3 minutes.

Bring the sugar and $^1/_4$ cup water to a boil in a small saucepan over medium-high heat. If sugar sticks to the sides of the pot, use a pastry brush dipped in water to clean it off. Once the mixture has boiled, add the corn syrup. Continue cooking until the sugar syrup turns a clear amber color, the edges begin to foam, and you can smell the caramel, about 10 minutes. Do not stir, or the sugar might crystallize.

Remove from the heat and immediately pour in the cream to stop the cooking process. Keep the pan away from you to avoid splatters. Whisk in the black pepper, pour the caramel into a container, and let it cool at room temperature for 2 hours. Remove the vanilla bean and rosemary, cover, then refrigerate for 12 to 24 hours. It can be kept covered and refrigerated for up to 2 weeks.

CARAMEL FILLINGS

I became inspired by the combination of *blood orange and caramel when I baked a wedding cake for my brother-in-law in Florida one spring and wanted to use the fruits as a nod to the location of the wedding. The acidity of the orange balances the sweetness of the caramel, which makes this filling perfect with Orange (page 77) or Cardamom (page 84) shells.*

Blood Orange Caramel

Makes 1½ cups, enough for 40 small sandwiched macarons

- ½ cup (120 grams) heavy cream
- ¼ cup (45 grams) freshly squeezed and strained blood orange juice (from 2 blood oranges)
- 2 packed tablespoons (26 grams) finely grated blood orange zest (from 2 blood oranges)
- 2 cups (400 grams) granulated sugar
- 1 teaspoon (4 grams) freshly squeezed and strained lemon juice (from ½ lemon)

Heat the cream, orange juice, and orange zest in a small saucepan over medium heat until it is scalding (almost to a boil), about 3 minutes.

Heat the sugar and lemon juice in a medium saucepan over medium heat. Stir with a wooden spoon or a heat-resistant spatula to "rub" the juice into the sugar until the sugar resembles wet sand. Cook until the sugar syrup *(continued)*

IMAGE ON LEFT: *Orange Shells with Blood Orange Caramel*

turns a clear amber color, the edges begin to foam, and you can smell the caramel, about 10 minutes. Stir only if the sugar does not melt evenly.

Remove from the heat and immediately pour in the cream to stop the cooking process. Keep the pan away from you to avoid splatters. Pour the caramel into a container, and let it cool at room temperature for 2 hours. Cover, then refrigerate for 12 to 24 hours. It can be kept covered and refrigerated for up to 2 weeks.

Coconut Caramel

Because it uses coconut milk rather than cream, this caramel is lactose-free. The coconut, vanilla bean, star anise, and ginger give it a spicy complexity that goes well with shells such as Ginger (page 85), Cocoa (page 75), or Vanilla (page 72).

MAKES 1½ CUPS, ENOUGH FOR
40 SMALL SANDWICHED MACARONS

½ cup (165 grams) unsweetened coconut milk, well-stirred
    (not cream of coconut)
2 cups (400 grams) granulated sugar
1 teaspoon (4 grams) freshly squeezed and
    strained lemon juice (from ½ lemon)
1 vanilla bean
1 whole star anise
1 (1-inch) piece fresh ginger, unpeeled and
    cut into ¼-inch slices

Heat the coconut milk, vanilla bean, star anise, and ginger in a small saucepan over medium heat until the mixture is scalding (almost to a boil), about 3 minutes.

Heat the sugar and lemon juice in a medium saucepan over medium heat. Stir with a wooden spoon or a heat-resistant spatula to "rub" the juice into the sugar until the sugar resembles wet sand. Cook until the sugar syrup turns a clear amber color, the edges begin to foam, and you can smell the caramel, about 10 minutes. Stir only if the sugar does not melt evenly.

Remove from the heat and immediately pour in the coconut milk and spices to stop the cooking process. Keep the pan away from you to avoid splatters and whisk well. Pour the caramel into a container, and let it cool at room temperature for 2 hours. Remove the vanilla, star anise, and ginger, cover, then refrigerate for 12 to 24 hours. It can be kept covered and refrigerated for up to 2 weeks.

This filling starts with raspberry jam to which

white chocolate and raspberry eau-de-vie are added; that jam is then combined with caramel. It can be used after two hours, without overnight refrigeration. The tartness of the raspberries keeps it from being too sweet—a risk anytime white chocolate is involved. I like to use it in Pistachio Shells (page 71) in the spring and summer; the jam is also terrific on its own, without the caramel.

Raspberry— White Chocolate Caramel

½ pint (170 grams) raspberries

1 cup (200 grams) granulated sugar, divided

5 ounces (160 grams) white chocolate, chopped

1 tablespoon (13 grams) framboise (raspberry eau de vie)

1 teaspoon (4 grams) freshly squeezed and strained lime juice (from ½ lime)

⅓ cup (80 grams) heavy cream

Clip a candy thermometer to a small, non-reactive stainless steel pot. Add the raspberries and ⅓ cup sugar and bring to a boil over medium-high heat, stirring constantly. Once the mixture reaches the boiling point, continues stirring until it reaches 220°F (105°C) on the thermometer and is spreadable, about 10 minutes. Remove from the heat, stir in the white chocolate, and then the framboise. Set aside while you continue with the recipe.

Heat the cream in a small saucepan over medium heat until it is scalding (almost to a boil), about 3 minutes.

Heat the remaining $^2/_3$ cup sugar and lime juice in a medium saucepan over medium heat. Stir with a wooden spoon or a heat-resistant spatula to "rub" the juice into the sugar until the sugar resembles wet sand. Cook until the sugar syrup turns a clear amber color, the edges begin to foam, and you can smell the caramel, about 5 minutes. Stir only if the sugar does not melt evenly.

Remove from the heat and immediately pour in the cream to stop the cooking process. Keep the pan away from you to avoid splatters. Stir in the raspberry-chocolate jam and pour the caramel into a shallow pan so that it can cool faster. Let it cool until it is thick and spreadable, about 2 hours. It can be kept covered and refrigerated for up to 2 weeks.

I live by the ocean, and spend most of my free summer nights strolling the boardwalk to enjoy the waves and the warmth as much as possible. Ice cream stores abound, many of which offer add-ins to mix into the flavors you select. I asked for apricots, ginger, and chocolate chips to accompany a scoop of caramel ice cream. The combination was so good that I had to develop it into a macaron filling. Pair it with Ginger (page 83), Cocoa (page 75), or simply with Almond (page 40) shells, since a lot of flavors are already involved. This caramel can be used two hours after making it.

Apricot-Ginger-Chocolate Caramel

MAKES 1¾ CUPS, ENOUGH FOR
40 SMALL SANDWICHED MACARONS

1 cup plus 2 tablespoons (270 grams) heavy cream

1¼ cups (213 grams) dried apricots, cut into quarters

1 tablespoon (16 grams) crystallized ginger, chopped

1 cup (200 grams) granulated sugar

1 teaspoon (4 grams) freshly squeezed and strained orange juice (from ½ orange)

5 ounces (160 grams) semisweet chocolate, chopped

Heat the cream and the apricots in a small saucepan over medium heat until the cream is scalding (almost to a boil), about 3 minutes. Let it stand for 15 minutes, to rehydrate the fruits, then transfer it to the bowl of a food processor or a blender, add the ginger, and purée until smooth. Set aside while you make the caramel.

Heat the sugar and lime juice in a medium saucepan over medium heat. Stir with a wooden spoon or a heat-resistant spatula to "rub" the juice into the sugar until the sugar resembles wet sand. Cook until the sugar syrup turns a clear amber color, the edges begin to foam, and you can smell the caramel, about 5 minutes. Stir only if the sugar does not melt evenly.

Remove from the heat and immediately pour in the cream mixture to stop the cooking process. Keep the pan away from you to avoid splatters. Stir in the apricot purée and chocolate, whisk until the chocolate is melted, then pour the caramel into a shallow pan so that it can cool faster. Let cool until it is thick and spreadable, about 2 hours. It can be kept covered and refrigerated for up to 2 weeks.

One of my favorite store-bought treats is the *chocolate caramels of La Maison du Chocolat. I developed the flavors into a perfect filling for macarons, which I like to pair with Cocoa (page 75) or Black Pepper (page 101) shells.*

Creamy Dark Chocolate Caramel

MAKES 1½ CUPS, ENOUGH FOR
40 SMALL SANDWICHED MACARONS

¾ cup (180 grams) heavy cream

2 cups (400 grams) granulated sugar

1 teaspoon (4 grams) freshly squeezed and strained lemon juice (from ½ lemon)

4 ounces (120 grams) bittersweet chocolate, chopped

1 teaspoon (3 grams) vanilla extract

Heat the cream in a saucepan over medium heat until scalding, about 3 minutes.

Heat the sugar and lemon juice in a medium saucepan over medium heat. Stir with a wooden spoon or a heat-resistant spatula to "rub" the juice into the sugar until the sugar resembles wet sand. Cook until the sugar syrup turns a clear amber color, the edges begin to foam, and you can smell the caramel, about 10 minutes. Stir only if the sugar does not melt evenly.

Remove from the heat and immediately pour in the cream to stop the cooking process. Keep the pan away from you to avoid splatters. Whisk in the chocolate and vanilla, pour the caramel into a container, and let it cool at room temperature for 2 hours. Cover, then refrigerate for 12 to 24 hours.

IMAGE ON LEFT: *Coconut Shells with Creamy Dark Chocolate Caramel*

FROZEN FILLINGS

ALMOND ICE MILK ✦ **ANISE ICE MILK**

✦ **ORANGE-BUTTERMILK ICE MILK** ✦

FUDGESICLE ✦ **HONEY FROZEN**

YOGURT ✦ **PERSIMMON ICE MILK**

✦ **CHAMOMILE ICE MILK**

THESE FROZEN FILLINGS WILL HAVE a better, creamier texture if you let them sit in the refrigerator for 24 hours before processing them in the ice cream maker. The sitting time allows for the hydration of the solids. But if pressed for time, you can process them as soon as the mixture is cooled to about 40°F (5°C).

When I worked at The Rainbow Room in New York, we were constantly catching a couple of waiters standing in the walk-in freezer, eating our frozen macarons. A frozen filling transforms a macaron into one tasty ice cream sandwich, whether you use store-bought products or make your own using one of the recipes in this chapter. These ice milks are designed for simplicity and speed—assuming you have an ice cream maker. An ice milk is easier to make than traditional custard-based ice cream, because there are no eggs to cook, and it is lighter for the same reason.

You can fill the shells in advance and freeze the macarons until ready to serve. They keep well that way, and can be served straight from the freezer. Each recipe should make enough to fill a batch of macaron shells—the exact yield will depend on your ice cream maker. You'll use more of a frozen filling than you'd use of another type, to make a thick ice cream macaron sandwich. Use a small, 1-inch (2.5 cm) ice cream scoop.

FILLING ICE CREAM SANDWICH MACARONS

WITH A MINI ICE-CREAM SCOOP, SCOOP THE FROZEN FILLING INTO 40 small, 1-inch macaron shells. Be gentle, to not break the shells. Top with another shell, pressing it down slightly. Return to the freezer until ready to serve. The macarons will keep up to 1 month in the freezer, wrapped tightly in plastic wrap.

This is a recipe that pastry chef Kurt Walrath *made when I worked at The Rainbow Room. It is light and refreshing, and makes for a simple, flavorful macaron when paired with Almond shells (page 40). Almond syrup is often called orgeat (if French made), or orzata (if Italian). You can find it in gourmet grocery stores, in coffee supply stores, and online (see Resources, page 257).*

Almond Ice Milk

MAKES 3 CUPS, ENOUGH FOR
40 SMALL SANDWICHED MACARONS

1¼ cups (375 grams) almond syrup
1¼ cups (285 grams) milk
¼ teaspoon (1 gram) vanilla extract
Pinch fine sea salt

Blend together the almond syrup, milk, vanilla extract, and salt in a blender until completely smooth, about 1 minute. You can also place all the ingredients in a bowl and blend with an immersion blender. Pour the mixture into an ice cream maker and process according to the manufacturer's instructions.

Transfer the almond ice milk to a freezer-safe container, cover, and freeze for at least 2 hours, up to 1 month.

This ice milk uses both anise seeds and star

anise, to make sure that the flavor fully comes out. I like to serve it as part of an assortment of macarons, which is a great way to get people to try more unusual flavors. Pair with Licorice (page 79) or Vanilla (page 72) shells.

MAKES 3 CUPS, ENOUGH FOR 40 SMALL SANDWICHED MACARONS

½ vanilla bean
½ cup (100 grams) granulated sugar
1½ cups (368 grams) half-and-half
2 tablespoons (16 grams) anise seeds
4 whole star anise
¼ cup (72 grams) light corn syrup

Anise Ice Milk

Split the vanilla bean in half lengthwise, and use the back of a paring knife to scrape out the seeds. Stir them into the granulated sugar, and rub the bean into the sugar to extract as many seeds as possible.

Bring the vanilla bean, sugar, half-and-half, anise seeds, star anise, and corn syrup to a boil in a small saucepan over medium-high heat, stirring to dissolve the sugar. Remove from the heat and infuse for 1 hour.

Strain the mixture. If it is not completely cool, refrigerate it for about 20 minutes. Pour it into an ice cream maker and process according to the manufacturer's instructions. Transfer the anise ice milk to a freezer-safe container, cover, and freeze for at least 2 hours, up to 1 month.

The buttermilk makes this ice milk slightly *tangy, and gives it a more interesting flavor than if you were to simply make orange ice milk. Pair this filling with Orange (page 77) or Almond (page 40) shells.*

Orange– Buttermilk Ice Milk

MAKES 3 CUPS, ENOUGH FOR
40 SMALL SANDWICHED MACARONS

1 cup (282 grams) buttermilk

¾ cup (180 grams) heavy cream

1 tablespoon (12 grams) freshly squeezed and strained lemon juice (from ½ lemon)

3 tablespoons (36 grams) freshly squeezed and strained orange juice (from 1 orange)

½ cup (100 grams) granulated sugar

1 tablespoon (13 grams) Grand Marnier

Blend together the buttermilk, cream, lemon juice, orange juice, sugar, and Grand Marnier in a blender until completely smooth, about 1 minute. You can also place all the ingredients in a bowl and blend with an immersion blender. Pour the mixture into an ice cream maker and process according to the manufacturer's instructions.

Transfer the orange–buttermilk ice milk to a freezer-safe container, cover, and freeze for at least 2 hours, up to 1 month.

Coffee leftover from breakfast will work well
here, even if it might stretch the definition of "freshly brewed" by a couple of hours. This filling tastes just like fudgesicles, especially when paired with Cocoa Shells (page 75).

Fudgesicle

MAKES 3 CUPS, ENOUGH FOR
40 SMALL SANDWICHED MACARONS

¼ cup (50 grams) granulated sugar
2 tablespoons (36 grams) light corn syrup
¼ cup (25 grams) cocoa powder
⅓ cup (90 grams) freshly brewed coffee
Pinch fine sea salt
1 cup (228 grams) milk
4 ounces (120 grams) milk chocolate, chopped
1 tablespoon (13 grams) dark rum

Bring the sugar, corn syrup, cocoa powder, coffee, salt, and milk to a boil in a medium saucepan over medium-high heat, whisking to dissolve the cocoa powder. When it reaches a boil, remove from the heat and add the chocolate and rum. Whisk thoroughly until smooth. Let cool to room temperature.

Transfer the chocolate mixture to a blender and blend until it's completely smooth, about 2 minutes. Pour the mixture into an ice cream maker and process according to the manufacturer's instructions.

Transfer the fudgesicle ice milk to a freezer-safe container, cover, and freeze for at least 2 hours, up to 1 month.

I like to use a honey that will reinforce the flavor of the macaron shells—for example, a lavender honey for Lavender Shells (page 89). Buckwheat honey is delicious with Lime (page 78) or Black Pepper (page 101) shells, and any honey will be a great match for Walnut Shells (page 68).

Honey Frozen Yogurt

MAKES 3 CUPS, ENOUGH FOR 40 SMALL SANDWICHED MACARONS

½ vanilla bean
1½ cups (357 grams) plain Greek-style yogurt
⅔ cup (220 grams) honey

Split the vanilla bean in half lengthwise, and use the back of a paring knife to scrape out the seeds.

Blend together the vanilla seeds, yogurt, honey, and ¾ cup (172 grams) water in a blender until completely smooth, about 2 minutes. You can also place all the ingredients in a bowl and blend with an immersion blender. Pour the mixture into an ice cream maker and process according to the manufacturer's instructions.

Transfer the yogurt mixture to a freezer-safe container, cover, and freeze for at least 2 hours, up to 1 month.

In North America, persimmons are typically available *from November to January. My grandfather had a tree in his backyard in rural Maryland, which I loved to visit when it was time to harvest the fruits. You will find two varieties: hachiya, which is astringent, and fuyu, which is not and looks almost like an orange tomato. Either will work for this recipe; just make sure that they are very ripe. So that the sweet, almost apricot-like flavor of the fruit can really shine, I usually pair it with Almond Shells (page 40).*

Persimmon Ice Milk

MAKES 3 CUPS, ENOUGH FOR
40 SMALL SANDWICHED MACARONS

3 (675 grams) ripe persimmons
½ cup (100 grams) granulated sugar
1 cup (245 grams) half-and-half
¼ cup (72 grams) light corn syrup
1 teaspoon (3 grams) vanilla extract
Pinch fine sea salt

Cut the persimmons in half, scoop out their flesh, and place it in a blender. Add the sugar, half-and-half, corn syrup, vanilla extract, and salt and blend until completely smooth, about 2 minutes. You can also place all the ingredients in a bowl and blend with an immersion blender. Pour the mixture into an ice cream maker and process according to the manufacturer's instructions.

Transfer the persimmon ice milk to a freezer-safe container, cover, and freeze for at least 2 hours, up to 1 month.

A student introduced me to this filling in *class one day; it's a delicate herbal flavor that is delicious with Marigold (page 88), Licorice (page 79), or Wasabi (page 103) shells.*

MAKES 3 CUPS, ENOUGH FOR
40 SMALL SANDWICHED MACARONS

¾ cup (150 grams) granulated sugar

¼ cup (72 grams) light corn syrup

1¾ cups (429 grams) half-and-half

2 packed tablespoons (8 grams) loose chamomile tea, or 4 tea bags

½ teaspoon (1.5 grams) vanilla extract

Pinch fine sea salt

Chamomile Ice Milk

Prepare an ice water bath by combining ice cubes and cold water in a bowl or pot. Bring the sugar, corn syrup, half-and-half, and tea to a boil in a small saucepan over medium-high heat, stirring to dissolve the sugar. Remove from the heat, let it infuse for 5 minutes, then strain out the tea, pressing to extract as much flavor from it as possible. Stir in the vanilla and salt and immediately place the pan over the ice water bath to chill completely, about 30 minutes.

Pour the mixture into an ice cream maker and process according to the manufacturer's instructions.

Transfer the chamomile ice milk to a freezer-safe container, cover, and freeze for at least 2 hours, up to 1 month.

IMAGE ON RIGHT: *Licorice, Wasabi, and Marigold Shells with Chamomile Ice Milk*

FRUIT-BASED FILLINGS

CINNAMON-APPLE BUTTER WITH CALVADOS ✶

PUMPKIN-SPICE BUTTER ✶ SOUR CHERRY COMPOTE

✶ GINGER-HONEY-PLUM COMPOTE ✶

APRICOT-VANILLA JAM ✶ WHITE PEACH JAM

✶ LEMON MARMALADE WITH CAMPARI

✶ CHILE-PINEAPPLE-KUMQUAT MARMALADE

✶ BLACKBERRY JELLY ✶ APRICOT-PASSION PÂTE DE FRUIT

✶ STRAWBERRY-GUAVA PÂTE DE FRUIT

✶ *Variation: Pear Pâte de Fruit*

Fruits are a great way to introduce seasonality in your macarons, since you can showcase the best flavors available at any given moment. I like a lot of variety in fillings, so these showcase a wide range of textures. Fruit butters do not contain dairy products; rather, they are a traditional, creamy-smooth American way to preserve fruit. Compotes are thicker and slightly chunky, and contain less sugar than jams or pâtes de fruits. Macarons with fruit-based fillings will not freeze well and should be consumed immediately.

Jams are fruits cooked with sugar, and pectin when needed, until they start gelling. The fruits are not strained out, so they are thicker than jellies, which are made with fruit juices. Marmalades are just as thick as jams, but typically refer to citrus-based products.

Pâtes de fruit (fruit paste) are a close relative of jams and jellies. They are cooked up to a higher temperature, which results in more water evaporating, and a tighter filling. They are often sold in confectionery shops cut into squares and rolled in granulated sugar to prevent sticking.

POURING FILLINGS INTO A SHALLOW PAN allows them to cool faster. You can use a casserole dish or a cake pan, for example.

FILLING WITH FRUIT

MOST OF THESE FILLINGS HAVE SOME TEXTURE TO THEM, OR CAN BE quite thick. For this reason, you will have an easier time using a spoon to fill the macaron shells rather than piping from a pastry bag. Spoon a small amount of the filling in a circular shape about $\frac{1}{2}$-inch thick, not going all the way to the edge, on the flat sides of 40 shells. Top with another shell, twisting slightly to secure the filling.

If you do not plan on using fruit fillings—other than pâtes de fruits—right away, you can pour them in an airtight container instead of a shallow pan and let them cool before refrigerating.

IF YOU DO NOT OWN A CANDY THERMOMETER, check the temperature of the jams, marmalades, jellies, and pâtes de fruit by dropping a few drops into ice water (use a heatproof spoon or spatula to do so). At 220°F (105°C), the drops should hold their shape in the water. At 225°F (107°C), the mixture will cling to the whisk while you are stirring. Jams are typically cooked to 220°F (105°C), which keeps them looser. If you like them firmer, cook them to 225°F (107°C).

Calvados is a French apple brandy. You can *substitute applejack (an American apple brandy) or plain brandy if you prefer. If you cannot find cider, use water or apple juice instead. Pair this filling with Almond (page 40) or Cinnamon (page 84) shells.*

5 medium apples (such as Golden Delicious, Granny Smith, and Fuji), cored and quartered

½ cup (120 grams) apple cider, divided

1 stick cinnamon

¾ packed teaspoon (3 grams) finely grated orange zest (from ½ orange)

1 packed cup (218 grams) light brown sugar

1 tablespoon (13 grams) Calvados

Simmer the apples and ¼ cup (60 grams) apple cider in a medium saucepan with a thick bottom on low heat until the apples are soft, about 20 minutes.

Press the cooked apples through a sieve to purée them and remove their skins.

Simmer the apple purée, remaining ¼ cup (60 grams) apple cider, cinnamon stick, orange peel, and sugar in a medium saucepan over medium-low heat, stirring constantly, until the mixture is thick and dark, about 20 minutes. It should be boiling gently, with big, wide steam bubbles, and coat the back of a spoon.

Remove from the heat, remove and discard the cinnamon stick, and stir in the Calvados. Let it cool completely. The butter can be kept covered and refrigerated for up to 2 weeks.

I love to include a lot of spices in my pump-kin pies, because the combination of cinnamon, ginger, cloves, and cardamom gives them heat and complexity. I follow the same principles in this pumpkin butter, with even more flavor added by apple cider. It pairs well with Ginger (page 85), Orange (page 77), or Walnut (page 68) shells. You can use canned or freshly made pumpkin purée, and substitute water or apple juice for the cider if it is not available.

Pumpkin— Spice Butter

MAKES 1 PINT, ENOUGH FOR
40 SMALL SANDWICHED MACARONS

2 cups (472 grams) pumpkin purée
¼ cup (60 grams) apple cider
¾ packed cup (164 grams) light brown sugar
1 teaspoon (2.75 grams) ground cinnamon
¾ teaspoon (1.5 grams) ground ginger
¾ teaspoon (1.75 grams) ground cardamom
¼ teaspoon (.5 gram) ground cloves
¼ teaspoon (1 gram) fine sea salt

Simmer the pumpkin purée, cider, sugar, cinnamon, ginger, cardamom, and cloves in a small saucepan over medium-low heat, stirring constantly, until the mixture is very thick and dark, about 20 minutes. It should be boiling gently, with big, wide steam bubbles, and coat the back of a spoon.

Remove from the heat, stir in the salt, and let cool completely. The butter can be kept covered and refrigerated for up to 2 weeks.

Cherry and almonds are a classic pairing
that makes this filling particularly delicious on Almond (page 40), Orange (page 77) or Cocoa (page 75) shells.

(page 40), Orange (page 77) or Cocoa (page 75)

MAKES 1 PINT, ENOUGH FOR
40 SMALL SANDWICHED MACARONS

2 cups (305 grams) dried sour cherries
1 stick cinnamon
2 (2-inch-long) strips orange peel
2 cups (400 grams) granulated sugar
1 cup (208 grams) red wine
1 tablespoon (12 grams) freshly squeezed
  and strained orange juice (from ½ orange)
Pinch freshly ground nutmeg

Sour Cherry Compote

Roughly chop the cherries in a food processor.

Bring the cinnamon stick, orange peel, sugar, wine, and orange juice to a boil in a medium saucepan over medium-high heat, stirring to dissolve the sugar. Reduce the heat to low and let simmer for 5 minutes, then remove the cinnamon and orange zest with a slotted spoon. Stir in the cherries.

Clip a candy thermometer to the pan, turn the heat back up to medium-high, and bring the mixture back to a boil. Let it cook, stirring constantly, until it reaches 220°F (105°C) and begins to gel. Stir in the nutmeg, then pour the mixture in a shallow pan and let it cool completely. The compote can be kept covered and refrigerated for up to 1 month.

Nick Malgieri, a colleague at the Institute

of Culinary Education, makes a roasted plum and ginger filling for galettes that inspired this filling. I added honey (a fairly mild flavor, such as wild-flower or clover, is best, so as to not overpower the other ingredients), black pepper, and Grand Marnier. The compote's beautiful purple color looks and tastes fantastic with Lemon (page 78), Black Pepper (page 101), or Vanilla (page 72) shells. It also makes a great yogurt topping for breakfast.

Ginger–Honey–Plum Compote

MAKES 1 PINT, ENOUGH FOR
40 SMALL SANDWICHED MACARONS

8 medium plums, unpeeled, cut into ½-inch pieces
1 cup (336 grams) honey
1 teaspoon (10 grams) freshly grated ginger (1-inch piece)
Pinch fine sea salt
Pinch freshly ground black pepper
2 tablespoons (26 grams) Grand Marnier

Bring the plums, honey, ginger, salt, and black pepper to a boil in a medium saucepan on medium heat, stirring to combine. Reduce the heat to low and cook for another 15 minutes, stirring constantly, until the juices thicken and the plums feel soft when probed with a knife. Stir in the Grand Marnier, then pour the mixture in a shallow pan and let it cool completely. The compote can be kept covered and refrigerated for up to 2 weeks.

This French-style jam is delicious on its own, but resist the urge to eat it all with a spoon and spread it in between Vanilla (page 72) or Blackberry (page 81) shells. You can also make it with fresh apricots in season: use about ten ripe apricots, peeled and quartered, and purée them until smooth.

Apricot–Vanilla Jam

MAKES 1 PINT, ENOUGH FOR
40 SMALL SANDWICHED MACARONS

½ vanilla bean

2 tablespoons (25 grams) granulated sugar

2½ cups (425 grams) dried apricots, cut into quarters

1 packed teaspoon (4 grams) finely grated orange zest (from 1 orange)

1 tablespoon (13 grams) Grand Marnier

Split the vanilla bean and scrape its seeds out by running the back of a knife over its length. Stir the seeds and the orange zest with the sugar.

Bring the apricots and 1½ cups (344 grams) water to a boil in a medium saucepan over medium-high heat. Remove from the heat and let sit for 30 minutes.

Clip a candy thermometer to the pan, stir in the orange sugar, and cook over medium heat, stirring constantly, until the mixtures reaches 220°F (105°C) or is spreadable, about 10 minutes.

Once ready, remove from the heat, stir in the Grand Marnier, pour the jam into a shallow pan and let it cool completely. It can be kept covered and refrigerated for up to 1 month.

Use gloves to handle the bird's eye chile, or *you will be sorry if you happen to rub your eyes later. It's a tiny but potent chile, commonly used in Thailand; you can substitute other types of red chiles. This marmalade takes longer to reach the right temperature because of the pineapple, which adds liquid. Pair it with Coconut (page 68), Lime (page 78), or Passion Fruit (page 83) shells.*

Chile—Pineapple—Kumquat Marmalade

MAKES 1 PINT, ENOUGH FOR
40 SMALL SANDWICHED MACARONS

½ vanilla bean
1½ cups (300 grams) granulated sugar
2 cups (300 grams) cubed fresh pineapple
  (from ½ large pineapple)
1 cup (185 grams) kumquats, cut into eights
1 bird's eye chile, seeded and finely chopped

Split the vanilla bean and scrape its seeds out by running the back of a knife over its length. Stir the seeds with the sugar, "rubbing" them all together so that they flavor the sugar.

Stir together the pineapple, kumquat, and sugar into a medium non-reactive stainless steel saucepan, and let macerate for 1 hour, until the fruits' juices are drawn out.

Clip a candy thermometer to the pan, add the chile, then cook the mixture, stirring constantly, over medium heat until it reaches 220°F (105°C) or is spreadable, about 20 minutes. The marmalade will thicken considerably as

it cools, so be careful to not overcook it.

Once ready, remove from the heat, stir in the lemon juice and salt, pour the jam into a shallow pan, and let it cool completely. It can be kept covered and refrigerated for up to 1 month.

Campari is an herb-based, slightly bitter liqueur that is highly recognizable thanks to its bright red color. Italians often serve it with an orange slice as garnish. In this filling, it complements the lemon flavor deliciously and gives the marmalade a pink hue that resembles pink lemonade. Pair with Lemon-Poppyseed (page 78), Pink Peppercorn (page 101), or Almond (page 40) shells. The preparation time is about two and a half hours, but for most of it you don't need to do anything, so you could make the macaron shells while waiting.

Lemon Marmalade with Campari

MAKES 1 PINT, ENOUGH FOR 40 SMALL SANDWICHED MACARONS

3 lemons (335 grams)
2 cups (400 grams) granulated sugar
1 tablespoon (13 grams) Campari
⅛ teaspoon (.5 gram) fine sea salt

Bring the lemons and enough water to cover them (about 1½ quarts) to a boil in a medium non-reactive stainless steel saucepan over medium-high heat. Drain, then cover with water again, and return to a boil. This reduces the bitterness of the lemons. Reduce the heat to low and simmer for 1 hour, then remove from the heat and let the lemons cool completely in the water.

Remove the cooled lemons from the pan, reserving the water in which they (continued)

IMAGE ON LEFT: *Orange Shells with Lemon Marmalade with Campari, Ginger-Plum Honey Compote and Orange Cream shown in background*

cooked. Cut them in half and discard their seeds. Finely chop the lemons then return them to the water, stir in the sugar, and cook on very low heat for 1 hour.

Clip a candy thermometer to the pan, turn the heat up to medium, and cook the mixture, stirring constantly, until it reaches 220°F (105°C) or is spreadable, about 10 minutes. The marmalade will thicken considerably as it cools, so be careful to not overcook it.

Once ready, remove from the heat, stir in the Campari and salt, pour the marmalade into a shallow pan, and let it cool completely. It can be kept covered and refrigerated for up to 1 month.

White peaches have a short season, but I find them to be the most flavorful variety of the fruit. They also have an ever-slightly pink hue where the skin meets the flesh, which gives this jam a very delicate color. You can use yellow peaches instead, of course, and even frozen ones. Pair it with Lime (page 78) or Almond (page 40) shells.

MAKES 1 PINT, ENOUGH FOR
40 SMALL SANDWICHED MACARONS

¾ teaspoon (2.25 grams) powdered pectin

1¼ cups (250 grams) granulated sugar

6 large ripe white peaches, peeled and cut into
  ½-inch pieces

1 packed teaspoon (4 grams) finely grated lime
  zest (from 1 lime)

1 teaspoon (4 grams) freshly squeezed and strained
  lime juice (from ½ lime)

White Peach Jam

Whisk the pectin into the sugar in a large non-reactive stainless steel saucepan so that it disperses evenly when cooking. Stir in the peaches and lime zest and let macerate for 1 hour, until the fruits' juices are drawn out.

Clip a candy thermometer to the pan and cook the mixture, stirring constantly, over medium heat until it reaches 220°F (105°C) or is spreadable, about 10 minutes.

Once ready, remove from the heat, stir in the lime juice, pour the jam into a shallow pan, and let it cool completely. It can be kept covered and refrigerated for up to 1 month.

As a child, I would go on long blackberry-*picking walks, pulling the ripe berries from thorny bushes and gently depositing them in my basket. My mom would then make pies or jams with our bounty. Pair this with Blackberry (page 81), or Coconut (page 68) shells. Use frozen berries when fresh ones are not in season.*

Blackberry Jelly

MAKES 1 PINT, ENOUGH FOR
40 SMALL SANDWICHED MACARONS

⅔ teaspoon (2 grams) powdered pectin

2¼ cups (450 grams) granulated sugar

1½ pints (510 grams) blackberries

1½ teaspoons (6 grams) freshly squeezed and strained lemon juice (from ½ lemon)

Pinch fine sea salt

Whisk the pectin into the sugar in a medium non-reactive stainless steel saucepan so that it disperses evenly when cooking. Stir in the blackberries and let macerate for 1 hour, until the fruits' juices are drawn out.

Bring the mixture to a boil over medium-high heat and let it boil for 5 minutes, stirring constantly. Clip a candy thermometer to the pan, reduce the heat to medium, then cook the mixture, stirring constantly, until it reaches 220°F (105°C) or is spreadable, about 10 minutes. The jelly will thicken considerably as it cools, so be careful to not overcook it.

Once ready, remove from the heat, stir in the lemon juice and salt, strain the jelly through a fine-mesh strainer (to get rid of the seeds), and let it cool completely. It can be kept covered and refrigerated for 1 month.

You will find apricot and passion fruit purée *in specialty food stores (we've also seen passion fruit purée in the frozen aisles of Latin grocery stores), but most easily online (see Resources, page 257). They are often sold frozen, so let them thaw out before use. You can make your own purée with fresh fruit: peel, pit, and purée them, then strain them through a fine-mesh sieve. Play up the passion fruit flavor by filling the matching shells (page 83), or use Coconut (page 68) or Almond (page 40) shells.*

Apricot–Passion Pâte de Fruit

MAKES 1 PINT, ENOUGH FOR
40 SMALL SANDWICHED MACARONS

1½ cups (360 grams) apricot purée

½ cup (120 grams) passion fruit purée

2 cups (400 grams) granulated sugar

¼ cup (72 grams) light corn syrup

1 teaspoon (4 grams) freshly squeezed and strained lemon juice (from ½ lemon)

Bring the apricot and passion fruit purées, sugar, and corn syrup to a boil in a medium non-reactive stainless steel saucepan over medium-high heat, stirring constantly. Reduce the heat to medium, clip a candy thermometer to the pan, and continue cooking the mixture, stirring constantly, until it reaches 225°F (107°C) or clings to the whisk, about 15 minutes. The fruits will darken while cooking, which is normal. The pâte de fruit will thicken considerably as it cools, so be careful to not overcook it.

(continued)

Remove from the heat, stir in the lemon juice, and pour the mixture in a shallow pan to cool completely until it is thick and set, about 2 hours. It will keep for 2 weeks, stored in an airtight container at room temperature or in the refrigerator. This filling will be too thick to pipe, so spoon small amounts of it onto the shells.

Guava is a sweet tropical fruit that often *has a bright pink flesh. You will find the paste in the Latin aisle of most grocery stores, sold in a round and flat container at very reasonable prices. I first started combining it with strawberries at Windows on the World, in a sorbet that had a beautiful pink-reddish hue and a deliciously sweet flavor. You can buy strawberry purée online (see Resources, page 257) or make your own with frozen berries: let them thaw, purée, and strain them through a fine-mesh sieve. Pair it with Strawberry (page 82) or Pistachio (page 71) shells.*

Strawberry—Guava Pâte de Fruit

MAKES 1 PINT, ENOUGH FOR
40 SMALL SANDWICHED MACARONS

¾ teaspoon (2.25 grams) yellow pectin (see note, page 203)
2 cups (400 grams) granulated sugar
1½ cups (400 grams) strawberry purée
1 cup (145 grams) guava paste

IMAGE ON RIGHT: *Strawberry Shells with Strawberry-Guava Pâte de Fruit*

¼ cup (72 grams) light corn syrup
1 teaspoon (4 grams) freshly squeezed and strained
lemon juice (from ½ lemon)

Whisk the pectin into the sugar in a medium non-reactive stainless steel saucepan so that it disperses evenly when cooking. Add the strawberry purée, guava paste, and corn syrup to a boil, stirring constantly. Clip a candy thermometer to the pan and continue cooking the mixture until it reaches 225°F (107°C) or clings to the whisk, about 15 minutes. The fruits will darken while cooking, which is normal. The pâte de fruit will thicken considerably as it cools, so be careful to not overcook it.

Remove from the heat, stir in the lemon juice, and pour the mixture in a shallow pan to cool completely until it is thick and set, about 2 hours. It will keep for 2 weeks, stored in an airtight container at room temperature. This filling will be too thick to pipe, so spoon small amounts of it onto the shells, evenly dividing it among them.

Variation: Pear Pâte de Fruit

You can buy pear purée online (see Resources, page 257). Poire Williams is a pear eau-de-vie that will increase the pear flavor of the pâte de fruit. Pair it with Cocoa (page 75), Hazelnut (page 68), Wasabi (page 103), or Almond (page 40) shells.

Use ½ teaspoon (1.5 grams) yellow pectin, replace the strawberry purée and guava paste by 2 cups (480 grams) pear purée, and stir in 1 tablespoon (13 grams) Poire Williams with the lemon juice.

YELLOW PECTIN

YELLOW PECTIN IS A SLOW-SETTING, NON-REVERSIBLE GELLING agent processed from citrus fruit or apples. It is used for jams, jellies, and pâtes de fruit, and works particularly well with fruits that have a higher water content, such as strawberries. You can order it online (see Resources, page 257). If you substitute regular pectin, the pâtes de fruit might set too loosely, which is not ideal for a macaron filling.

FAVORITE AMERICAN CLASSICS

GERMAN CHOCOLATE CAKE ✦

RED VELVET CAKE ✦ CARROT CAKE ✦

DULCE DE LECHE ✦ KEY LIME

WITH MARSHMALLOW FLUFF ✦

✦ TROPICAL PIÑA COLADA ✦ S'MORES ✦

This chapter features beloved American desserts in macaron form, which also gives them the advantage of being gluten-free. Making those macarons for friends who can't enjoy the real thing will earn you a healthy supply of friendship points. Because some involve several components, they require a little more time than "regular" macarons but you will find them to be well worth any additional effort.

Take this idea of using two fillings and don't be afraid to experiment with other flavors and to mix and match as you please. It's a great way to use up leftover filling, for example.

TO ASSEMBLE THESE MACARONS, spoon each filling into a pastry or resealable plastic bag, and cut a $^1/_2$-inch opening at the tip. Pipe it on 40 shells, top with the second filling if there is one, and then with another shell. When filling shells with two different flavors, you need to pipe or spoon a smaller amount of each filling so as not to overfill. Refrigerate for up to 2 days before serving, and let the macarons come to room temperature before serving. You can refrigerate or freeze any leftover filling as indicated.

Serving German chocolate cake as a bite-size *treat makes for a surprising dessert. Use this filling with Pecan (page 68) or Cocoa (page 75) shells.*

German Chocolate Cake

MAKES 1 PINT, ENOUGH FOR
40 SMALL SANDWICHED MACARONS

½ cup (150 grams) unsweetened condensed milk
½ cup (100 grams) granulated sugar
6 tablespoons (84 grams) unsalted butter
2 egg yolks, whisked
¾ cup (6.5 grams) sweetened coconut flakes
½ cup (60 grams) pecan pieces, finely chopped
Pinch fine sea salt
1 teaspoon (3 grams) vanilla extract

Bring the condensed milk, sugar, and butter to a boil in a small saucepan over medium-high heat. Reduce the heat to medium and stir in the yolks, coconut flakes, pecans, salt, and vanilla extra. Continue cooking, stirring continuously, until the mixture thickens and begins to boil. It will darken because of the caramelization of the sugar, which is perfectly normal.

Pour the mixture into a shallow pan and let it cool to lukewarm, about 15 minutes. If it cools completely it will be harder to handle. Spoon it into the shells immediately.

IMAGE ON LEFT: *Cocoa and Pecan Shells with German Chocolate Cake Filling*

Red velvet is the quintessential Southern

cake. Its red color initially came only from a reaction between baking soda and cocoa powder, but nowadays red food coloring is added to most versions, for a brighter color. Many red velvet cakes are filled and frosted with a cream cheese buttercream (only some recipes call for this, others use a milk-based, cooked cream. Here, the macarons are filled with a cream cheese fluff.

Red Velvet Cake

MAKES 40 SMALL SANDWICHED MACARONS

4 ounces (120 grams) cream cheese, room temperature
½ stick (56 grams) unsalted butter, softened
½ packed cup plus 1 tablespoon (125 grams) confectioners' sugar
1 teaspoon (3 grams) vanilla extract
Pinch fine sea salt
1 recipe Red Velvet Shells (page 76)

In the bowl of an electric mixer fitted with the paddle attachment, beat together the cream cheese and butter on low speed until the mixture is fluffy, about 4 minutes.

Add the confectioners' sugar, vanilla extract, and salt. Beat until smooth, about 5 minutes, scraping regularly with a spatula to ensure that everything is well combined. The fluff can be kept covered and refrigerated for up to 1 week. Spoon it into a piping bag when ready to fill.

Pipe a small amount of the cream cheese filling in a circular shape about ½-inch thick, not going all the way to the edge, on the flat sides of 40 of the shells. Top with another shell, twisting slightly to secure the fillings.

Dulce de leche is traditionally cooked down
from milk, and the sugars caramelize with slow cooking. This is an easy ver-
sion that starts with canned milk. This recipe is very rich; you won't need
much to fill each macaron, thus the smaller yield. It pairs well with Lime
(page 78), Cinnamon (page 84), or Cashew (page 68) shells.

MAKES 1 CUP, ENOUGH FOR
40 SMALL SANDWICHED MACARONS

1 (14-ounce or 396-gram) can sweetened condensed milk
Pinch baking soda
Pinch fleur de sel
1 teaspoon (3 grams) vanilla extract
1 recipe Lime (page 78), Cinnamon (page 84),
  or Cashew (page 68) shells

Dulce
de
Leche

Preheat the oven to 400°F (205°C). Set a kettle of water to boil.

Stir together the condensed milk, baking soda, fleur de sel, and vanilla extract in an 8-inch cake pan, and cover it with aluminum foil. Place the pan in a larger casserole dish, transfer it to the oven, and pour enough boiling water into the larger dish to reach halfway up the sides of the pan. Bake for $3\frac{1}{2}$ hours, until it has thickened and has turned a deep caramel color. If the water bath evaporates while the dulce de leche cooks, add more hot water as necessary.

Remove from the oven and let cool completely. Spoon the filling into a piping bag, and pipe onto the shells. This dulce de leche can be kept covered and refrigerated for up to 2 weeks.

Halwa is a dense, sweet confection found *primarily in the Middle East and in Asia. Pastry chef Anil Rohira offered carrot halwa as part of his featured dessert when Dessert Professional named him one of its Top Ten Pastry Chefs of the year, which inspired me to turn it into a carrot cake-like filling for a macaron. The texture of this filling resembles shredded carrots, and its flavor is that of carrot cake.*

Carrot Cake

MAKES 40 SMALL SANDWICHED MACARONS

CARROT HALWA

1 (14-ounce or 400-gram) can condensed milk, divided

2 tablespoons (16 grams) powdered milk

3 medium carrots, peeled and coarsely grated

2 tablespoons (40 grams) golden raisins, finely chopped

1 tablespoon (20 grams) candied pineapple, finely chopped

$\frac{1}{8}$ teaspoon (.25 gram) ground cardamom

$\frac{1}{4}$ teaspoon (.7 gram) ground cinnamon

Pinch ground cloves

Pinch fleur de sel

GRAND MARNIER CREAM CHEESE FLUFF

2 ounces (60 grams) cream cheese, room temperature

2 tablespoons (28 grams) unsalted butter, softened

$\frac{1}{2}$ packed teaspoon (2 grams) finely grated orange zest (from $\frac{1}{2}$ orange)

$1\frac{1}{2}$ teaspoons (7 grams) Grand Marnier

Pinch fleur de sel

1 recipe Cinnamon Shells (page 84)

For the carrot halwa: put 2 tablespoons (28 grams) of condensed milk into a small bowl. Stir in the powdered milk until the mixture is smooth, and set aside.

Cook the carrots and remaining condensed milk in a medium saucepan over medium heat for about 20 minutes, stirring occasionally. The carrots will start rendering their juices after about 10 minutes. Once the liquid is half reduced, about 5 minutes later, stir in the raisins, pineapple, cardamom, cinnamon, and cloves. Continue cooking, stirring gently until the liquid is mostly evaporated, about 5 more minutes.

While the carrots are cooking, prepare an ice water bath for the saucepan.

Stir the powdered milk mixture and fleur de sel into the carrots, then remove from the heat and immediately place over the ice water bath to cool. The halwa can be kept covered and refrigerated for up to 1 week. Do not freeze it.

For the cream cheese fluff: in the bowl of an electric mixer fitted with the paddle attachment, beat together the cream cheese and butter until the mixture is fluffy, about 4 minutes.

Add the orange zest, Grand Marnier, and salt. Beat until smooth, about 5 minutes, scraping regularly with a spatula to ensure that everything is well combined. The fluff can be kept covered and refrigerated for up to 1 week. Spoon it into a piping bag before using.

Spoon a small amount of the halwa in a circular shape about $^1/_4$-inch thick, not going all the way to the edge, on the flat sides of 40 of the shells. Pipe $^1/_4$-inch-thick dab of fluff on top of the halwa and top with another shell, twisting slightly to secure the fillings.

These macarons combine lime curd and *marshmallow, just like a real Key lime pie. The small torch sold as part of a crème brûlée kit works perfectly to torch the marshmallow filling. You can also buy one separately at a kitchenware or hardware store. But fret not: you can skip the torching and still have a great flavor.*

Key Lime with Marshmallow Fluff

MAKES 40 SMALL SANDWICHED MACARONS

½ vanilla bean

½ cup (100 grams) granulated sugar

2 egg whites

2 teaspoons (8 grams) freshly squeezed and strained key lime juice (from 1 key lime)

¾ packed teaspoon (3 grams) finely grated key lime zest (from 1 key lime)

½ teaspoon (1.5 grams) vanilla extract

1 recipe Lime Shells (page 78)

½ recipe Key Lime Curd (page 150)

Fill a pot over which the bowl of your electric mixer can fit without touching the bottom with about 2 inches of water. Bring the water to a boil over high heat, then reduce the heat to an occasional simmer.

Split the vanilla bean in half lengthwise, and use the back of a paring knife to scrape out the seeds. Stir them into the granulated sugar, and rub the bean into the sugar to extract as many seeds as possible.

(continued)

IMAGE ON RIGHT: *Lime Shells with Key Lime Curd and Marshmallow Fluff*

Put the egg whites, sugar, key lime juice, key lime zest, and vanilla extract in the bowl of an electric mixer (without setting it on the mixer just yet). With a hand whisk, whisk together to combine, then place the bowl over the pot of water and clip a candy thermometer to the bowl. Whisk until the mixture reaches 145°F (63°C).

Take the bowl off the heat and place it on the mixer. Fit the whisk attachment, and whisk at medium speed until glossy stiff peaks form and the mixture is very thick, about 7 minutes. Remove the vanilla bean, and spoon the marshmallow filling into a piping bag to pipe it immediately.

Spoon or pipe a small amount of the key lime curd in a circular shape about $^1/_4$-inch thick, not going all the way to the edge, on the flat sides of 40 of the lime shells. Pipe a $^1/_4$-inch-thick dab of marshmallow over the curd, and with a small torch, lightly torch the top of each marshmallow mound (if it catches on fire, blow on it!). Top with another shell, twist it slightly to secure the fillings, and serve immediately.

Coconut shells will give you the flavor of
a creamy cocktail and Caribbean night.

½ vanilla bean

¾ cup (150 grams) granulated sugar

⅓ teaspoon (1 gram) powdered pectin

2 cups (300 grams) cubed fresh pineapple
   (from ½ large pineapple)

Pinch fine sea salt

1 recipe Coconut Shells (page 68)

½ recipe Passion Fruit Pastry Cream (page 155)

Tropical
Piña
Colada

Split the vanilla bean in half lengthwise, and use the back of a paring knife to scrape out the seeds. Stir them into the granulated sugar, and rub the bean into the sugar. Whisk in the pectin.

Cook the pineapple in a medium non-reactive saucepan over medium-high heat for 10 minutes, stirring constantly. Reduce the heat to medium, clip a candy thermometer to the pan, stir in the sugar-pectin mixture and salt, and cook, stirring constantly, until it reaches 220°F (105°C) or is spreadable, about 20 minutes. The jam will thicken considerably as it cools, so don't overcook it. Pour the jam into a pan and let it cool. Cover and refrigerate for up to 2 weeks.

Spoon or pipe a small amount of jam in a circular shape about ¼-inch thick, not going all the way to the edge, on the flat sides of 40 of the shells. Pipe a ¼-inch-thick dab of pastry cream over the ganache, top with another shell, twist it slightly, and serve immediately.

S'more macarons are a great way to use left-
over ganache. *If you don't have any, make a half batch of your favorite recipe
(pages 104 to 127). For a very quick version, you can always use Nutella.*

S'mores

MAKES 40 SMALL SANDWICHED MACARONS

2 egg whites
½ cup (100 grams) granulated sugar
½ teaspoon (1.5 grams) vanilla extract
½ recipe any flavor ganache
1 recipe Cocoa (page 68) or Cinnamon (page 84) shells

Fill a pot over which the bowl of your electric mixer can fit without touching the bottom with about 2 inches of water. Bring the water to a boil over medium heat.

Put the egg whites, sugar, and vanilla extract in the bowl of an electric mixer (without setting it on the mixer just yet). With a hand whisk, whisk together to combine, then place the bowl over the pot of water and clip a candy thermometer to the bowl. Whisk until the mixture reaches 145°F (63°C).

Take the bowl off the heat and place it on the mixer. Fit the whisk attachment, and whisk at medium speed until glossy stiff peaks form and the mixture is very thick, about 7 minutes. Spoon the filling into a piping bag immediately.

Spoon or pipe a small amount of ganache in a circular shape about ¼-inch thick, not going all the way to the edge, on the flat sides of 40 shells. Pipe a ¼-inch-thick dab of marshmallow over the ganache, and with a small torch, lightly torch the top of each marshmallow mound. Top with another shell, twist it slightly to secure the fillings, and serve immediately.

IMAGE ON LEFT: *Cinnamon Shells with Crunchy Cacao Nib Ganache and Marshmallow Fluff*

SAVORY FILLINGS

HUMMUS ✦ CHÈVRE-ROSEMARY ✦

MUSHROOMS AND WHITE WINE ✦

MAPLE-BACON-BOURBON ✦ THAI CHILE-PEANUT ✦

TOMATO CONFIT ✦ CHICKEN MOLE ✦

FOIE GRAS WITH BLACK CURRANT GASTRIQUE ✦

✦ DUCK CONFIT WITH PORT AND FIG ✦

My sweet macaron classes at the Institute of Culinary Education are so popular that I had to think of ways to expand the offerings. A savory macaron class made a lot of sense, since they are perfect hors d'oeuvres to serve at a party, or even as an amuse-bouche (an appetizer before a meal) for a sit-down dinner. These recipes will give you a new way to experience not only macarons, but a wide range of flavor combinations.

BECAUSE THEY ARE THICK AND TEXTURED, most of these savory fillings should be spooned onto macaron shells rather than piped. Spoon a small amount of filling (evenly dividing it to have enough for all the shells) not going all the way to the edge, on the flat sides of 40 shells. Top with another shell, twisting it slightly to secure the filling. None of these fillings should be frozen, so it's best to prepare and assemble these macarons just before serving. You can make the shells ahead of time, freeze them, and bring them to room temperature before filling them.

These macarons offer a unique alternative

to the hummus bowl that has become ubiquitous at most parties as the veg-
etarian offering. Hummus pairs well with Sesame Shells (page 102), and
with Pink or Black Peppercorn (page 101) shells. Look for tahini in the Mid-
dle Eastern aisle of your supermarket. I like my hummus quite lemony, and
always squeeze extra lemon juice in case I want to add more later. You can
do the same here, but just make sure that the finished hummus is not too
runny, since it has to hold its shape in a macaron.

Hummus

MAKES 1 PINT, ENOUGH FOR
40 SMALL SANDWICHED MACARONS

2 whole heads garlic

3 tablespoons (39 grams) extra-virgin olive oil, divided

2 (15.5-ounce or 439-gram) cans chickpeas

¾ cup (195 grams) tahini

3 tablespoons (36 grams) freshly squeezed and strained
   lemon juice (from 1½ lemons), plus more to taste

1 teaspoon (2 grams) ground cumin

1 teaspoon (4 grams) fine sea salt, plus more to taste

Finely ground black pepper to taste

Preheat the oven to 375°F (190°C). Cut a piece of foil large enough to cover
both heads of garlic.

   Cut both heads of garlic in half horizontally, without peeling them, to
expose the tips of the cloves. Drizzle 2 tablespoons (26 grams) of the olive

oil on the foil, and place the heads of garlic on top of the oil (cut-side down so that they can absorb it as much as possible). Wrap the foil around them completely, then place on a baking sheet and bake for about 45 minutes, or until the heads feel very soft when probed with a knife. Remove them from the oven and let them cool completely.

Drain the chickpeas, reserving the liquid. Combine the chickpeas, tahini, lemon juice, cumin, and 1 teaspoon of salt in the bowl of a food processor or blender and process until the mixture is smooth.

Squeeze the cooled garlic cloves out of their skins and add them to the chickpea mixture, along with the remaining 1 tablespoon (13 grams) of olive oil. Process until well incorporated. Taste, and if necessary, adjust the texture with some of the reserved chickpea liquid. Season with more salt and black pepper to taste. This hummus can be kept covered and refrigerated for up to 4 days.

YOU CAN PIPE SMOOTHER FILLINGS like Hummus (page 220) or Chèvre-Rosemary (page 222), if you prefer: spoon the filling into a pastry or resealable plastic bag, and cut a $1/2$-inch opening at the tip.

The Mediterranean flavors of this creamy, *rich cheese mixture pair well with Walnut (page 68), Hazelnut (page 68), or Parsley (page 77) shells. Chèvre is fresh goat cheese, which you will find in the cheese case of your supermarket or at any cheese store.*

MAKES 1 PINT, ENOUGH FOR
40 SMALL SANDWICHED MACARONS

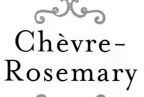

Chèvre-Rosemary

1 medium head garlic

1 tablespoon (13 grams) extra-virgin olive oil

1 small sprig (about 2 inches long) rosemary

1 (11-ounce or 305-gram) log fresh goat cheese

1 cup (225 grams) crème fraîche

¼ teaspoon (1 gram) fine sea salt, plus more to taste

¼ teaspoon (1 gram) coarsely ground black pepper, plus more to taste

Preheat the oven to 375°F (190°C). Cut a piece of foil large enough to cover the head of garlic.

Cut the head of garlic in half horizontally, without peeling it, to expose the tips of the cloves. Drizzle the olive oil on the foil, and place the head of garlic on top of the oil (cut-side down so that it can absorb it as much as possible). Wrap the foil around it completely, then place on a baking sheet and bake for about 45 minutes, or until the head feels very soft when probed with a knife. Remove it from the oven and let it cool completely. Once cool, squeeze the cloves out of the skin with your hands.

Remove the leaves from the rosemary sprig and chop them very finely. You should have about 1 teaspoon.

Place the chèvre, rosemary, and roasted garlic in the bowl of a stand mixer fitted with the paddle attachment, and mix at medium speed until the mixture is homogenous. Turn the mixer to low, add the crème fraîche, and mix until incorporated. Taste and season with the salt and pepper, adding more if you prefer. This filling can be kept covered and refrigerated for up to 4 days.

The earthy flavors of this mushroom filling *work particularly well with Hazelnut Shells (page 68)—probably because they are used to sharing forest floors. It is delicious regardless of the types of mushrooms you use, but keep in mind that some have more pronounced tastes than others (button and Portobello mushrooms are milder than morels and chanterelles, for example).*

Mushrooms and White Wine

MAKES 1 PINT, ENOUGH FOR 40 SMALL SANDWICHED MACARONS

1 quart (230 grams) assorted mushrooms (button, oyster, Portobello, shiitake, or morel)

2 tablespoons (26 grams) extra-virgin olive oil

2 tablespoons (28 grams) unsalted butter

1 tablespoon (30 grams) thinly sliced shallot (from 1 large shallot)

(continued)

1/8 teaspoon (.5 gram) ground cumin

1/4 cup (60 grams) dry white wine

1/2 teaspoon (2 grams) fine sea salt, plus more to taste

1/4 teaspoon (1 gram) freshly ground black pepper,
   plus more to taste

2 tablespoons (5 grams) parsley leaves, washed and
   finely chopped (from about 2 stalks)

Rinse and trim the mushrooms, removing their stems. Slice the mushroom caps into 1/8-inch pieces.

Heat the olive oil and butter in a wide sauté pan over medium-high heat. Add the shallots and cumin, and cook, stirring, until the shallots are a light golden color, about 5 minutes. Add the mushrooms, wine, salt, and pepper. Reduce the heat to medium-low and cook for about 15 minutes, stirring occasionally, until the liquid rendered by the mushrooms evaporates. Stir in the parsley, taste, and add salt and pepper if desired.

Spoon a small amount of the filling on 40 macaron shells and top with another shell. Serve warm or at room temperature.

This filling is deliciously spicy, but the heat
*is tempered by the peanut butter. I use Huy Fong Foods Chili Garlic Sauce,
which I find at my local supermarket. They also make sriracha, which you
can use instead if you prefer, but it doesn't contain any garlic so the flavor
will be slightly different. Chiles and peanuts are a classic Thai flavor combination that is furthered emphasized by using this filling with Ginger (page
85) or Lime (page 78) shells. It is rich, so use sparingly.*

Thai Chile–Peanut

**MAKES 1¼ CUPS, ENOUGH FOR
40 SMALL SANDWICHED MACARONS**

2 packed teaspoons (20 grams) peeled and freshly
grated fresh ginger (2-inch piece)

1 teaspoon (15 grams) finely chopped garlic
(from about 2 cloves)

1 tablespoon (12 grams) freshly squeezed and
strained lime juice (from ½ lime)

1 cup (240 grams) crunchy peanut butter

2 tablespoons (20 grams) soy sauce

2 teaspoons (10 grams) chile sauce

2 tablespoons (26 grams) rice vinegar

1 teaspoon (7 grams) honey

2 tablespoons (12 grams) scallion (from about 2
small stalks, white and green parts), finely sliced

Heat the ginger, garlic, lime juice, peanut butter, soy sauce, chili paste, vinegar, and honey in a small saucepan over medium-low for 5 minutes. Stir a few
(continued)

times while the ingredients are heating up to make sure everything is combined.

Taste the mixture and add more of any of the ingredients if desired. Remove from the heat, stir in the scallions, and immediately spoon the filling onto 40 macaron shells, evenly dividing it. Top with another shell, and serve warm or at room temperature.

BECAUSE OF THE SOY SAUCE, this is the only recipe in this book that is not completely gluten-free. Substitute a gluten-free variety if desired.

Tomato Confit

Anne came back from a trip to Spain with savory crackers bought at the famed Hoffman pastry shop in Barcelona, in between which was sandwiched a very richly flavored tomato confit. We ate them with such pleasure during a working session for this book that we decided to include a related filling. The smooth purée has the texture of tomato paste and an aroma redolent of summer, with olive oil and lemon thyme mellowing into the tomatoes during the cooking process. Because of its intense flavor, you don't need to use as much filling in each macaron. Use it with Saffron (page 98), Black Pepper (page 101), or Parsley (page 97) shells.

MAKES 1½ CUPS, ENOUGH FOR
40 SMALL SANDWICHED MACARONS

(continued)

IMAGE ON RIGHT: *Sesame Shells with Tomato Confit*

8 (about 2½ pounds or 1150 grams) ripe plum tomatoes

2 tablespoons (26 grams) extra-virgin olive oil

1 sprig lemon thyme, leaves only

¼ teaspoon (1 gram) coarse sea salt

¼ teaspoon (1 gram) coarsely ground black pepper

Prepare an ice water bath by combining ice cubes and cold water in a bowl or pot, then bring 2 quarts (1.8 liters) of water to a boil over high heat.

Cut out the stem end and score an "X" in the skin of each tomato. Plunge them in the boiling water for 30 seconds each, then immediately remove them and plunge them into the ice water bath. This will allow the skin to slip off easily. Let the tomatoes cool slightly, then cut them in half lengthwise and scoop out the seeds with a spoon.

Preheat the oven to 250°F (120°C).

Line a baking sheet with parchment paper or a silicone baking mat, and sprinkle the olive oil on top of it. Place the tomatoes cut-side down on the olive oil and sprinkle them with the thyme leaves, salt, and pepper. Bake for 1½ hours, until caramelized and soft if probed with a knife.

Transfer the tomatoes, oil, and seasonings to the bowl of a food processor and pulse 3 times to make a smooth purée. Scrape the sides of the bowl with a rubber spatula once during the process, to make sure that nothing sticks to the sides. Pipe the filling warm or let it cool to room temperature. It can be kept covered and refrigerated for up to 1 week.

Mole is a Mexican sauce that includes a
*variety of chiles, spices, and chocolate. A slew of regional variations exist,
not to mention the twists each cook might give a family recipe. Because it
contains so many aromatics, it has a very complex flavor—at times spicy,
at times sweet; you don't need too much filling in each macaron for it to
come through. Don't be intimated by the long ingredient list; each quantity
is small, which makes for a rather short preparation time. To accentuate
the taste of chocolate in the recipe, pair this filling with Cacao Nibs Shells
(page 75) to play up the chocolate, or on Ancho Shells (page 102) to bring
up its spiciness. Use a Microplane zester to grate the chocolate.*

Chicken Mole

MAKES 1½ CUPS, ENOUGH FOR
40 SMALL SANDWICHED MACARONS

½ teaspoon (1 gram) ground cumin

⅛ teaspoon (.5 gram) ground ancho chile powder

¼ teaspoon (.75 gram) ground cinnamon

¼ teaspoon (1 gram) fine sea salt

2 (3-ounce or 85-gram each) boneless chicken breasts,
   cut into ½-inch slices

1 tablespoon (13 grams) olive oil

1 tablespoon (30 grams) finely chopped onion
   (from ¼ small onion)

½ teaspoon (8 grams) finely chopped garlic
   (from 1 small clove)

(continued)

2 tablespoons (24 grams) freshly squeezed and strained
  orange juice (from ½ orange)

½ cup (120 grams) chicken stock

½ cup (140 grams) crushed plum tomatoes

1 teaspoon (5 grams) canned chipotle peppers, finely chopped

¼ packed teaspoon (1 gram) finely grated orange zest

½ ounce (14 grams) unsweetened chocolate, finely grated

2 tablespoons (42 grams) honey

Fine sea salt and freshly ground black pepper to taste

Mix the cumin, ancho chile, cinnamon, and salt in a small bowl to create a dry rub. Place the chicken slices in the bowl and coat them with the rub.

Heat the olive oil in a small sauté pan over medium-high heat. Add the chicken slices and cook for about 2 minutes, until they are seared. Turn them over and sear the other side for about 2 minutes. Transfer the chicken to a plate.

Add the onions to the pan and stir until they become translucent, about 1 minute. Add the garlic, then pour the orange juice and chicken stock into the pan to deglaze it. Reduce the heat to medium, add the tomatoes and chipotle peppers, and cook until the sauce thickens enough to coat the back of a wooden spoon, about 5 minutes.

While the sauce thickens, cut the chicken into ⅛-inch cubes. Once the sauce is ready, stir in the orange zest and chocolate until the chocolate is melted and reduce the heat to low. Add the chicken cubes and honey, and stir until the chicken is warmed through, about 4 minutes. Taste and season with salt and pepper as desired. Spoon the mole filling onto 40 macarons shells, evenly dividing it, then top with another shell, twist it slightly to secure the filling, and serve warm.

I ate foie gras with black currant gastrique

at Le Favre d'Anne, a Michelin-starred restaurant in Angers, France, when I was there on a trip with students. The taste was so memorable that I had to turn it into a filling for Black Pepper Shells (page 101). Foie gras is often served with a fruit-based condiment, but those can be too sweet and make the dish cloying. A gastrique—a sweet and sour vinegar reduction—adds tartness to balance the sweetness, and cuts through the richness of foie gras. You can buy foie gras lobes in gourmet grocery stores and online, and black currant purée online (see Resources, page 257).

Foie Gras with Black Currant Gastrique

MAKES 1½ CUPS, ENOUGH FOR
40 SMALL SANDWICHED MACARONS

½ cup (100 grams) granulated sugar

½ cup (105 grams) balsamic vinegar

1 tablespoon (13 gram) extra-virgin olive oil

1 teaspoon (10 grams) finely chopped shallot
(from 1 small shallot)

4 ounces (120 grams) foie gras, deveined and
sliced into ½-inch slices

2 tablespoons (26 grams) red wine

½ cup (120 grams) black currant purée

Fine sea salt and freshly ground black pepper to taste

Heat the sugar in a small saucepan over medium heat until it turns a golden

(continued)

caramel color, about 5 minutes. Remove the pan from the heat and carefully stir in the vinegar to stop the caramelizing process. Set aside while you cook the foie gras.

Heat a wide sauté pan over high heat. Add the olive oil and the shallots, and stir for 30 seconds. Add the foie gras slices and sear on one side for 45 seconds. Use a spatula to flip them over and sear the other side for another 45 seconds.

Remove the foie gras from the pan to a plate. Pour any excess fat into a bowl and reserve, then pour the red wine and black currant purée into the pan to deglaze it. Stir in the caramel, turn the heat to low, and let the liquid reduce until it coats the back of a wooden spoon, stirring occasionally, about 15 minutes. Stir in 1 tablespoon (13 grams) of the reserved foie gras cooking fat. Taste and season as desired with salt and pepper.

Immediately place a small piece of the seared foie gras onto 40 macaron shells. Drizzle a bit of gastrique over each, then top with another macaron shell and serve warm or at room temperature.

IMAGE ON LEFT: *Black Pepper Shells with Foie Gras with Black Currant Gastrique*

Duck confit is duck that has been preserved
*in its own fat. I like using D'Artagnan's, which you will find in most gourmet
grocery stores, but any type of duck confit, especially homemade, will do
(see Resources, page 257, if you want to order it online). Duck goes well
with sweet accompaniments, such as prunes and figs. The spices prevent
the filling from being too sweet here. Pair it with Orange (page 77) or Hazelnut (page 68) shells. You can use the port-fig filling on its own with sweet
shells, without duck, or with Orange Buttermilk Ice Milk (page 178).*

Duck Confit with Port and Fig

MAKES 1 PINT, ENOUGH FOR
40 SMALL SANDWICHED MACARONS

1 bay leaf

6 black peppercorns

2 sticks cinnamon

3 whole cloves

1 (2-inch-long) strip orange peel

⅔ cup (134 grams) granulated sugar

1 cup (225 grams) port

5 ounces (140 grams) dried figs,
  stems removed and cut in quarters

1 (3- to 4-ounce or 100- to 120-gram)
  piece duck confit, meat removed from
  the leg bone and cut into thin pieces

Wrap the bay leaf, peppercorns, cinnamon sticks, cloves, and orange peel in cheesecloth (you'll need 6 to 8 inches), bringing the four corners of the cloth together and tying them into a knot so that the spices do not spill. It should look like a small pouch. You can also place all the ingredients in a large tea ball.

Stir together the sugar and the port in a small saucepan over medium-high heat, and add the figs and spice pouch. Bring to a boil, then reduce the heat to low and let the mixture simmer for 20 minutes.

Preheat the oven to 300° F.

Drain the figs, reserving the liquid and discarding the spice pouch. Put the figs in the bowl of a food processor and pulse about 4 times for 3 seconds each, until you have a smooth fig compote. Scrape the sides between pulses. Taste, and add some of the spiced port liquid if needed. The compote should be soft enough to pipe, but not so liquid that it will run.

Place the duck confit pieces on a baking sheet, cover them with foil, and heat until warm, 6 to 8 minutes.

Spoon a dollop of fig compote on 40 macaron shells. Top with a piece of duck confit, then another macaron shell, and serve at room temperature or while the duck is still slightly warm.

The sweet and smoky flavors of bacon, bourbon, and maple syrup make this filling one of the most addictive of the book. It pairs well with a bourbon-based drink, as you can imagine, and other dark cocktails. Use it to fill Walnut (page 68), Orange (page 77), or Cocoa (page 75) shells. Use small dabs for a less slippery macaron.

MAKES 1½ CUPS, ENOUGH FOR
40 SMALL SANDWICHED MACARONS

12 ounces (340 grams) bacon, preferably nitrate-free, sliced thinly
2 tablespoons (24 grams) freshly squeezed and strained orange juice (from ½ orange)
2 tablespoons (42 grams) maple syrup
1 tablespoon (13 grams) bourbon
Pinch freshly ground black pepper

Maple-Bacon-Bourbon

Line a large plate with paper towels.

Cook the bacon in batches in a sauté pan over medium-high heat until it is crispy, 8 to 10 minutes. Remove the strips to the lined plate and let cool enough to handle, then finely chop the bacon.

Cook the orange juice, maple syrup, bourbon, and chopped bacon in a wide sauté pan over medium heat until warm, about 2 minutes, stirring frequently to ensure that nothing sticks to the bottom of the pan. Remove from the heat, and immediately spoon the filling onto 40 macaron shells, evenly dividing it. Top with another shell, twisting it slightly to secure the filling, and serve warm or at room temperature.

IMAGE ON LEFT: *Walnut Shells with Maple-Bacon-Bourbon Filling*

FOR LESS-THAN-PERFECT MACARONS

★ SARAH BERNHARDTS

★ OPEN-FACE FRESH FRUIT MACARON TARTS

★ CHOCOLATE BEEHIVES ★ TRIFLE

Macarons don't always come out perfectly. Even in one batch where most of them are perfect, some might be less so. Don't be discouraged—they are, first and foremost, delicious on their own as regular cookies. But there are also a number of desserts that you can make, some simple and some slightly more involved, with less-than-perfect macarons.

These recipes call for 40 shells—half a batch—because presumably not all of your finished macarons will be misshaped. They can be further divided to make smaller quantities based on the number of shells you may want to "disguise," and the amount of filling you have on hand.

History has it that a Danish pastry chef in-
*vented these cookies to celebrate famed nineteenth-century French ac-
tress Sarah Bernhardt. The crispy texture of the macaron, the soft
ganache, and the rich chocolate shell of this petit four undoubtedly evoke
beauty and luxury. This recipe is perfect for shells that are cracked or that
don't have feet as well formed as others. Tempering the chocolate before
dipping the petits fours in it gives it a snap once it cools, as well as a shiny
color. If you choose to not temper the chocolate, your Sarah Bernhardts
will still taste delicious but will look slightly less polished.*

Sarah Bernhardts

MAKES 40

1 recipe of your favorite ganache (pages 104 to 119),
   firm enough to pipe
40 Rose (page 91) or Almond (page 40) shells
1 recipe Tempered Chocolate (recipe follows)

Line a baking sheet with parchment paper.

Fill a pastry bag with the ganache and cut off a $^1/_2$-inch tip. Pipe a small amount of ganache, about $^1/_2$-inch thick, in a cone-like shape about 1 inch high, on the flat sides of the shells. Don't let the ganache go all the way to the edges of the macaron. Let the ganache set in the fridge, about 10 minutes.

Dip the ganache part of the cookies only in tempered chocolate (see page 242). The macaron base should remain chocolate-free. Place them on the parchment-lined baking sheet after dipping, then refrigerate for 10 minutes so that the chocolate sets. Store at room temperature for 2 days, in an airtight container in the refrigerator for up to 2 weeks, and in the freezer for up to 1 month.

Tempered Chocolate

Tempering consists of gradually lowering the temperature of couverture chocolate—a type of chocolate that contains a higher percentage of cocoa butter—through stirring, then slightly raising it again, to form a crystal structure in the chocolate that allows it to be shiny and solid at room temperature and "snap" crisply when you bite into it or break it into pieces. It's hard to temper small quantities of chocolate, so you will have a lot of it leftover. Let it solidify, and retemper when needed.

> 1 pound (453 grams) semisweet chocolate couverture, chopped (see page 257)

Fill a pot over which the bowl of your electric mixer can fit without touching the bottom with about 2 inches of water. Bring the water to a boil over high heat, then reduce the heat to maintain a simmer.

Put the chocolate in the bowl of an electric mixer. Place the bowl over the pan, clip a candy thermometer to the side of the bowl, and let melt until the chocolate reaches 115°F (46°C).

Take the bowl off the heat and set it on the mixer. Fit the paddle attachment, and beat at low speed until the chocolate reaches 84°F (29°C) on the candy thermometer.

Dip a piece of parchment paper in the chocolate, then let it set in the freezer for 5 minutes to see if the chocolate snaps (breaks cleanly). If it does, reheat the chocolate slightly over the simmering water for 8 to 10 seconds, until it reaches 88°F (31°C) on the candy thermometer. If the chocolate doesn't snap, continue to cool it in the mixer until a retest on parchment paper does snap.

Immediately use the chocolate to make the Sarah Bernhardts. If it starts to set, heat it briefly again over the simmering water for 10 seconds, and stir it again before using. Repeat the parchment test if you think it might have become too warm.

These tarts are a great way to try your hand *at making larger macarons. It takes about half the amount of any base macaron recipe to make eight 3-inch macarons. Prepare the recipe as you would for smaller macarons, but use the large size baking instructions (page 39). Ginger (page 85) or Green Tea (page 86) shells work well with the fruits used here, but feel free to substitute your favorite seasonal fruits and shell flavors, as well as store-bought ice cream.*

Open-Face Fresh Fruit Macaron Tarts

MAKES 8 (3-INCH) TARTS

8 (large, 3-inch) macaron shells of desired flavor and color, cooled

1 mango, peeled, cored, and sliced lengthwise into ⅛-inch-thick pieces (about 1½ cups of fruit)

1 pint (226 grams) strawberries, hulled and cut into ⅛-inch-thick pieces (about 1½ cups of fruit)

½ pint (170 grams) blackberries

2 tablespoons (40 grams) apricot jelly

1 tablespoon (13 grams) Grand Marnier

½ recipe of your favorite frozen filling (pages 174)

With the shells flat-side up on a workspace, arrange an assortment of fruits on top of each. Leave a 1-inch space for the sorbet slightly off center of the shells.

Heat the apricot jelly and Grand Marnier in a heat-proof container in the microwave for about 1 minute, until the mixture is spreadable. With a pastry brush, brush the mixture over the fruits to glaze them.

Using a 1½-inch ice cream scoop, top each tart with a scoop of sorbet and serve immediately.

I used to pipe "beehives" of leftover mousse *on cookies, sprinkle them with cocoa powder and decorate them with "bees" made of almonds. They would sell out every afternoon when mothers came into the bakery where I worked with their kids after school. Try this version made with macarons; the beehive will cover up a cracked shell and turn a failed macaron into a delicious treat.*

Chocolate Beehives

MAKES 40

1 recipe of your favorite ganache, or leftover ganache (pages 104 to 127), firm enough to pipe

40 macaron shells

¼ cup (25 grams) Dutch-processed cocoa powder

40 whole almonds, toasted (see page 135)

½ teaspoon (3 grams) vegetable oil

1 ounce (30 grams) semisweet chocolate pieces, melted (see page 125)

80 sliced blanched almonds

Fill a pastry bag with the ganache, and cut a ¼-inch opening at the tip. Working quickly so it will not set, pipe the ganache in a spiral on the base of a macaron shell, starting in the center. Continue building the spiral vertically, going back toward the center, in a beehive shape. Sprinkle the cocoa powder over the beehives, and refrigerate them briefly while working on the almond bees.

Arrange the toasted almonds on a cookie rack. Stir the oil in the melted chocolate. With a fork, quickly drizzle the chocolate over the almonds, to

(*continued*)

FOR LESS-THAN-PERFECT MACARONS

create the stripes of a bee. Refrigerate for 10 minutes, until set.

Position the bee bodies anywhere you want on the beehives, pressing each down slightly into the ganache so it stays in place. Press an almond slice on each side of each bee body to form the bee's wings. The beehives can be kept, refrigerated in an airtight container, for up to 1 week.

Trifles are a great way to make use of broken *macaron shells, since they will be hidden by pastry cream and jam or marmalade. You can make this dessert in one big bowl or serve it individually—small water glasses work well for that purpose, since they reveal the layers of the trifle. Some of the flavor combinations I like are Passion Fruit Pastry Cream (page 155) with Chile-Pineapple-Kumquat Marmalade (page 196); and Popcorn Pastry Cream (page 153) with Ginger-Honey-Plum Compote (page 190). But I encourage you to experiment with a variety of flavor and color combinations. You can use leftover Marshmallow Fluff (page 217) instead of whipped cream, if you prefer—a little will go a long way in this already-sweet dessert.*

Trifle

SERVES 8

1 cup (240 grams) heavy whipping cream
2 tablespoons (25 grams) granulated sugar
40 macaron shells, whole, misshapen, or broken
1 recipe of your favorite pastry cream (page 128)
(*continued*)

1 recipe of your favorite fruit filling (page 184)

1 pint (340 grams) raspberries or your favorite fruits

2 tablespoons (26 grams) of your favorite brandy, rum,
   or other spirit (optional)

Put the cream and the sugar in the bowl of an electric mixer fitted with the whisk attachment and whip on medium-high speed until stiff peaks form, about 8 minutes. Set aside.

Arrange one layer of macaron shells at the bottom of a clear glass bowl (I use a 7^3/$_4$- by 4^1/$_2$-inch or 20-by 12-cm trifle bowl) or distributed among 8 small glasses. Spoon one-third of the pastry cream over the macarons, then one-third of the fruit filling and one third of the raspberries. Sprinkle some brandy if using. Repeat until you have used up all the ingredients. Spoon or spread the whipped cream over the top. Let the trifle sit for a day if you can resist, covered and refrigerated, before serving to allow the flavors of all the layers to combine.

TROUBLESHOOTING GUIDE

Macarons have a reputation for being troublesome. Because so many variables can affect the finished product, it can take a few tries to make perfectly smooth shells. Even the most established chefs admit that they have bad macaron days, and pastry shops try to have the same (experienced) baker make them every day.

When you make macarons for the first time, pipe and bake just a couple once your batter is ready. This will allow you to troubleshoot any oven or batter issues before baking the full batch.

Most problems can be traced to your oven and how it bakes. To a lesser extent, measuring issues play a role in inconsistent results. And last, weather matters, too—humid days, for example, make it more difficult to obtain perfect macarons. This section allows you to troubleshoot a particular issue you may encounter.

A lot of what happens between a successful and unsuccessful batch is very subtle. It helps if you bake macarons often. Modify one variable at a time so that you know what technique is working for you and what factors are not.

The results listed below are possible results, not necessarily inter-related. In other words, one situation can have multiple effects.

Ingredient Measuring–Related Issues

SCENARIO A: **Too much almond flour**
RESULT 1: Excessive browning
RESULT 2: Sliding of shell off feet
RESULT 3: Batter too stiff
REMEDY: Measure more accurately, using a scale.

SCENARIO B: **Too much egg white**
RESULT 1: Very weak shell and/or air pocket under shell, fragile macaron
REMEDY: Age egg whites longer and/or add powdered egg white to reinforce the protein structure
RESULT 3: High dome rises in the center of shells and cracking occurs
REMEDY: Lower the amount of powdered egg white by half and the oven heat (follow the alternate baking instructions, page 256).

SCENARIO C: **Too much powdered sugar or granulated sugar**
RESULT 1: Misshapen shells with uneven explosions in shapes
RESULT 2: Excessive browning (from caramelization of sugars)
REMEDY: Measure more accurately, using a scale.

SCENARIO D: **Not enough sugar**
RESULT 1: No feet form around the shell
REMEDY: Increase the amount of granulated sugar by 1 tablespoon (13 grams).

Problems Related to Mixing or Piping

SCENARIO A: **Whipping time too long**
(egg white peaks don't form in 10 minutes or so)
RESULT 1: Feet too large
RESULT 2: Cracking
REMEDY: Whip the meringue for fewer minutes, either using a higher
speed on an electric stand mixer, or a wider bowl if whipping by hand.
When there is a lot of humidity in the air, the meringue can take
longer to form; increase the mixer speed slightly. If the air is very dry,
overwhipping might take place more easily; stop the mixer more frequently to check.

SCENARIO B: **Folding time too long**
RESULT: Cracking
REMEDY: Check more frequently while incorporating the dry ingre-
dients into the meringue for the exact degree of macaronnage.

SCENARIO C: **Dry ingredients not ground finely and powdery enough after sifting**
RESULT: Rough, misshapen shells
REMEDY: Purchase commercially ground almond flour; pulse more
times when combining it with confectioners' sugar, and sift more
times; practice and squeeze very hard when piping.

SCENARIO D: **Baking sheets not slammed enough after piping, before baking, to remove all the extra air from the batter**
RESULT: Air pocket inside shell
REMEDY: Slam the sheets vigorously.

SCENARIO E: **Batter too stiff**
RESULT: Tails, or points, on shell
REMEDY: Measure all the ingredients using a scale, for more accuracy; squeeze the batter out of the piping bag and immediately refill it; wait 1 hour before piping the batter (the hydration of dry ingredients improves), covering it with plastic wrap during that time.

OVER-MACARONNER

If you fold the batter for too long, the macarons may spread and have poorly shaped shells and feet. Your batter might also look really wet. If the batter is completely loose and too liquid, you will have trouble piping the right shapes and the macarons will be too flat. The next time, fold less.

UNDER-MACARONNER

Not incorporating the dry ingredients enough might result in a meringue that is too strong to allow the formation of the feet and popped-up crust that characterize macarons. The tops of the shells could also be lumpy. If the shells hold their shapes after piping and do not settle into a smooth surface, you will have "tails" (or peaks) in the center of the macarons after baking them. You need to fold a few more times, or what you will bake will be more of a meringue cookie than a macaron. If you've been doing so (folding more than 10 more times) and the batter still hasn't loosened, spoon the batter into the piping bag, then squeeze it out and immediately refill the bag.

Troubleshooting the Baking Process

SCENARIO A: **Shell too strong, too dry**
RESULT: Batter doesn't know where to go, spreads outward
REMEDY: Bake quicker (follow the alternate baking instructions, page 256), at higher initial heat to reduce the drying time.

SCENARIO B: **Oven heat too low, shell too weak**
RESULT 1: Batter remains wet too long, steam forms cracks in the shell
RESULT 2: Too chewy, egg proteins cooked too long
REMEDY: Bake on fewer baking sheets (bake a test batch of 2 shells to see), so that more heat can penetrate the shell.

SCENARIO C: **Oven heat too high, shell cooks too quickly**
RESULT 1: Excessive browning of shell (and possibly, raw/chewy interior, if took the macarons out of the oven too soon)
REMEDY: Prop the oven door open with a wooden spoon two-thirds of the way into the baking process.
RESULT 2: Air pocket under the shell; batter (under the shell) sticks to the silicone baking mat or the parchment paper after the shell has risen off its feet
REMEDY: Bake on lower heat for additional time (follow the alternate baking instructions, page 236) for a more even process; use fewer baking sheets.
RESULT 4: Shell not shiny, dull appearance

REMEDY: Whip the meringue fewer minutes (when the meringue is whipping properly, it will be shiny and glossy); bake immediately at the higher temperature, without drying the shells at 200°F (95°C); try the Italian meringue method; freeze the finished shells, unwrapped, for 1 hour.

SCENARIO D: Uneven oven heat
RESULT 1: Sloped shell or "baseball cap" effect
REMEDY: Rotate the baking sheets twice, and not just back to front but also top to bottom of the oven.
RESULT 2: Convex hollow space at the bottom of the baked shell (these tend to form if the shell cooks too quickly in an unevenly heated oven)
REMEDY: Use an additional baking sheet to disperse the heat.
RESULT 3: Cracks form only on some shells (often on the perimeter of the baking sheet)
REMEDY: Rotate the baking sheets more frequently.

SCENARIO E: Low oven heat
RESULT 1: Excessive sliding of shell from its feet and/or feet too wide
RESULT 2: Possible chewiness of macaron
RESULT 3: Wrinkles, darkness, and/or indentations on top of shell
REMEDY: Get more initial heat into the shell by following alternate baking instructions (see page 256); use fewer baking sheets; close the oven door quickly if you rotate the baking sheets.

SCENARIO F: Shells are difficult to remove, and have a dark or sunken center in the shell

REMEDY 1: Bake on fewer baking sheets, and use alternate baking instructions to get more heat into the shells (page 256).

REMEDY 2: Freeze baked shells on the silicone baking mat or parchment paper for 2 hours before removal, or let them sit on the pan 24 hours at room temperature, then carefully slide a metal offset spatula under each shell to remove it, applying downward pressure to not crack it.

REMEDY 3: Switch to a silicone baking mat.

Oven Temperature Issues
and Alternate Baking Instructions

If the correct amount of time has elapsed but the centers of your shells look either compressed or darker than the edges, leave them in 1 to 2 more minutes or they will be so underbaked that you won't be able to remove them from the baking sheet. Macarons crisp up upon cooking, so don't overbake the shells or they will be dry. Look for firmness in the edges of the shell around the foot. If your shells are always funny-shaped, you need to bake on more baking sheets to help disperse the oven heat. Using a silicone baking mat and piping the shells with firm pressure can help too. If you have a convection oven, decrease the temperature in a recipe by 25 to 35 degrees.

If it appears to run too hot (no feet form on the shells, typically), pipe the macarons and bake at 325°F for 10 minutes, rotating the pan after 3 minutes and 6 minutes.

If it appears to run too low (the batter "explodes," creating bursts in the shells and uneven shapes), pipe the macarons and bake at 425°F for 3 minutes; rotate the baking sheets front to back, reduce the heat to 325°F, and bake for another 6 minutes. Return the oven to its original temperature before baking each new batch.

These instructions should help for small (1-inch) shells; larger and cocoa shells will need longer baking times.

RESOURCES

The companies listed here are primarily wholesalers who sell to the public and retail outlets. The wholesalers may be new companies to you, but they are where chefs shop. Some will require a minimum order, but if you need more than one item it may be economical. You might also find it worth it to buy certain items in bulk. You may save quite a bit of money by buying a larger quantity of commercially processed almond flour, for example, dividing it up in freezer-safe resealable plastic bags, and storing it in your freezer.

AMAZON
www.amazon.com
(800) 201-7575
Amazon sells nearly anything you will need to make macarons, from baking equipment like baking sheets, silicone mats, and digital scales to specialty ingredients like dried unsweetened flaked coconut, matcha, orzata, and powdered egg whites.

AMERICAN ALMOND PRODUCTS COMPANY
www.americanalmond.com
(800) 825-6663
This wholesale company sells nuts and nut flours in 5- and 25-pound boxes.

AMORETTI
www.amoretti.com
(800) 266-7388 or (805) 983-2903
This company offers a large selection of flavor compounds, as well as essential and citrus oils and almond flour.

ATLANTIC SPICE COMPANY

www.atlanticspice.com
2 Shore Road, Truro, MA
(508) 487-6100
Great source for parsley powder and edible flower petals such as rose and lavender.

AUI (ALBERT USTER IMPORTS)

www.auiswiss.com
(800) 231-8154
This long-time supplier to chefs around the country sells almond flour, powdered fruits and licorice powder, specialty baking ingredients such as chocolates, cacao nibs, flavor compounds, fruit purées, vanilla beans, and praline paste.

CHEF RUBBER

www.shopchefrubber.com
(702) 614-9310
A good resource for unusual food colorings, including powders, as well as equipment such as digital scales.

THE CHEFS' WAREHOUSE

www.chefswarehouse.com
(718) 842-8700

Another industry supplier that sells to the public, this company supplies almond flour and specialty baking ingredients such as powdered egg whites, chocolates, cacao nibs, fruit purées, vanilla beans, and praline paste.

D'ARTAGNAN

www.dartagnan.com
(800) 327-8246
The products of this specialty meats company, including duck confit and foie gras, are available in gourmet food shops nationwide and online.

L'EPICERIE

www.lepicerie.com
(866) 350-7575
L'Epicerie sells smaller quantities of ingredients previously sold only wholesale. It offers powdered fruits and licorice powder, nut flours, praline paste, fruit purées, flavor compounds, pure natural flavors, essential and citrus oils, and other specialty baking ingredients.

JB PRINCE

www.jbprince.com
36 E. 31st Street, New York, NY
(800) 473-0577
This equipment retailer sells baking
sheets, piping bags and tips, and silicone
baking mats.

KEREKES

www.bakedeco.com
6103 15th Avenue, Brooklyn, NY
(718) 232-7044
You will find there a large assortment of
unusual food colorings, including powders, and other equipment such as parchment paper and piping bags.

KING ARTHUR FLOUR

www.kingarthurflour.com
135 US Rt. 5 South, Norwich, VT
(800) 827-6836
This miller of fine flours is a great source
for almond flour, pearl sugar, almond
paste, and other baking ingredients.

NY CAKE & BAKING DISTRIBUTORS

www.nycake.com
56 W. 22nd Street, New York, NY

(212) 675-2253
and NY Cake West
10665 W. Pico Boulevard, Los Angeles,
CA 90064
(310) 481-0875
This New York institution now also has a
location in Los Angeles, and ships all over
the world. It sells food colorings, chocolates, pearl sugar, specialty baking ingredients, and equipment such as baking
sheets, silicone baking mats, parchment
paper, and piping bags and tips.

PARIS GOURMET

www.pastrygourmet.com
(800) PASTRY-1
Another good source for almond flour,
chocolates, fruit purées, vanilla beans,
and other specialty ingredients.

PFEIL & HOLING

www.cakedeco.com
58-15 Northern Boulevard, Woodside, NY
(800) 247-7955
This cake decorating company supplies
food colorings, including powders, and
equipment such as piping bags and tips.

SUGARPASTE/CRYSTAL COLORS

www.sugarpaste.com
574-233-6524
This company offers a beautiful assortment of unusual food colorings.

TRADER JOES

www.traderjoes.com
You will find almond flour, chocolates, and other common baking and cooking ingredients at your local branch of this national retailer.

WHOLE FOODS, LOCAL BRANCHES

www.wholefoodsmarket.com
You will find almond flour and other common baking and cooking ingredients at your local branch of this national retailer.

ACKNOWLEDGMENTS

FROM KATHRYN AND ANNE:

We first need to thank the millions of people around the world who love macarons and have made them popular enough that we could write a book about them, and the pastry chefs who tirelessly make them, innovating with flavors, fillings, and decoration techniques and provide us with such inspiration.

We are grateful to our agent, Jennifer Griffin, for having found the perfect home for this project. She was a supporter and an advocate every step of the way.

Our editor, Kristen Green Wiewora, and art director, Amanda Richmond, are as passionate about macarons as we are, which made them the perfect companions for this journey. All authors should be so lucky to find such champions for their project. Kristen's thoughtful and attentive editing resulted in improvements every step of the way. Thank you also to copy editor Alice Sullivan.

Please visit us online: Kathryn's website is www.moulinbregeon-cuisinecourses.com, and Anne's website is www.potsandplumes.com.

FROM KATHRYN:

Many friends were instrumental in the development of this book:

Kurt Walrath, the pastry chef who taught me how to make macarons (using Meilleur Ouvrier de France Pascal Brunstein's macaron method).

Hervé Poussot, another former boss at Le Bernardin and Windows on the World, who really understands macarons as the chef-owner of Almondine.

New York pastry chefs Eric Bedoucha (chef-owner of Financier) and Richard Capezzi (formerly at Bouchon Bakery) for allowing me into their production facilities and providing assistance with macaron walking tours and high-volume production techniques.

Pastry chefs Stephan Iten and Stéphane Glacier, MOF for their help over the years troubleshooting macarons during the annual World Pastry Forum.

My professional colleagues and friends, pastry chefs Jeff Yoskowitz and Tina Körting, for help brainstorming and pushing me to expand my knowledge of macaron baking procedures.

Anne, whom I got to know better in the course of this project, for her diligent research and seemingly tireless efforts during the writing process.

Rick Smilow, the president of the Institute of Culinary Education (ICE), who generously let me test recipes there.

The myriad of ICE alumni and students, and macaron lovers encountered along the way, particularly Ed DeLandri, Trevor Hardwick, Shelly Lee Goldberg, and Michele Friedman, who helped me teach hands-on macaron classes, test shell recipes in their home ovens, and deepen my knowledge of this subject.

My partner Jessie Riley, who turned out to be the ultimate recipe tester and food stylist.

FROM ANNE:

I am grateful to have had the opportunity to collaborate with Kathryn on this project. She is one of the most hard-working and thorough people I have ever met, and made writing this book with her an absolute pleasure and constant source of learning and inspiration.

My husband, Ron McBride, patiently ate all the macarons I fed him, no matter what time of day or his appetite. I am forever thankful for both his loving support and his balanced meals.

My family in Switzerland and France gave me the love of good food, and that includes good pastry. I can't think of a better homage to that than a book on macarons.

Cesar Vega, food scientist extraordinaire, was a ready consultant for all matters of technical questions. Every conversation taught me much and resulted in engaging exchanges.

Jackie Rohel was a willing recipe tester as well as an encouraging and welcoming ear throughout the process, as were Meryl Rosofsky, Tae Ellin, and Courtney Knapp, and all the friends who humored lengthy macaron-related discussions.

Fabio Parasecoli provided quick and able etymological assistance, including translation, with his usual generosity.

INDEX

Note: Page references in *italics* indicate photographs.

A

Almond flour
  about, 16
  buying and storing, 16
  Cocoa Shells, *74*, 75
  Cocoa Shells with Cacao Nibs, 75
  drying, 17
  French Meringue Method, 40–44
  Italian Meringue Method, 45–50
  Kathryn's Easiest French Macaron Method, 55–58
  making your own, 67
  Red Velvet Shells, 76
  Swiss Meringue Method, 51–54
Almond(s). *See also* Almond flour
  -Cherry Cream, 156
  Chocolate Beehives, *244*, 245–246
  Ice Milk, 176
  -Lemon Cream, 157
  Shells, 40
American classics
  about, 205
  Carrot Cake Filling, 209–210
  Dulce de Leche Filling, 209
  German Chocolate Cake Filling, 206, 207
  Key Lime with Marshmallow Fluff Filling, 212–214, *213*
  Red Velvet Cake Filling, 208
  S'mores Filling, *216*, 217
  spooning or piping onto shells, 205
  Tropical Piña Colada Filling, 214–215
Ancho Chile Shells, 102
Anise Ice Milk, 177
Apple-Cinnamon Butter with Calvados, 187
Apricot-Ginger-Chocolate Caramel, 170–171

B

Apricot-Passion Pâte de Fruit, 199–200
Apricot-Vanilla Jam, 191
Bacon-Maple-Bourbon Filling, *236*, 237
Base recipes (Almond shells)
  French Meringue Method, 40–44
  Italian Meringue Method, 45–50
  Kathryn's Easiest French Macaron Method, 55–58
  Swiss Meringue Method, 51–54
Basil Buttercream, 136–138, *137*
Beehives, Chocolate, *244*, 245–246
Blackberry Jelly, 198
Blackberry Shells, 81, *152*
Black Currant Gastrique with Foie Gras Filling, 231–233, *232*
Black Pepper Shells, *100*, 101
Blood Orange Caramel, *164*, 165–166
Bourbon
  -Maple-Bacon Filling, *236*, 237
  -Pumpkin Buttercream, 143–144
Brittle, Sesame, 140
Buttercreams
  Basil, 136–138, *137*
  freezing, 129
  Gingerbread, 144
  Maple, 133
  meringue-based, about, 129
  Oatmeal Cookie, 141–142
  piping onto shells, 130
  Pistachio, 134–135
  Pumpkin-Bourbon, 143–144
  Sesame, 139–140
  Vanilla, *87*, 131–132
Buttermilk-Orange Ice Milk, 178

C

Cacao Nib Ganache, Crunchy, *106*, 107
Cacao Nibs, Cocoa Shells with, 75
Calvados, Cinnamon–Apple Butter with, 187
Campari, Lemon Marmalade with, *194*, 195–196
Caramel fillings
    Apricot-Ginger-Chocolate, 170–171
    Blood Orange, *164*, 165–166
    Coconut, 166–167
    Creamy Dark Chocolate, *172*, 173
    Fleur de Sel, 160–162, *161*
    making ahead, note about, 162
    making caramel for, 159
    piping onto shells, 159
    Raspberry–White Chocolate, 168–169
    Rosemary, 162–163
Cardamom Shells, 84
Carrot Cake Filling, 209–210
Cashew Shells, 68
Cassis
    Foie Gras with Black Currant Gastrique,
        231–233, *232*
    –White Chocolate Ganache, *93*, 124–125
Chai Ganache, 119–121, *120*
Chamomile Ice Milk, 182, *183*
Cheese. *See* Chèvre; Cream cheese
Cherry, Sour, Compote, 189
Cherry-Almond Cream, 156
Chèvre-Rosemary Filling, *96*, 222–223
Chicken Mole Filling, 229–230
Chickpeas
    Hummus Filling, 220–221
Chile(s)
    Ancho, Shells, 102
    Chicken Mole Filling, 229–230
    -Pineapple-Kumquat Marmalade, 192–193
Chocolate. *See also* White Chocolate
    -Apricot-Ginger Caramel, 170–171
    Beehives, *244*, 245–246
    Chai Ganache, 119–121, *120*

Chicken Mole Filling, 229–230
Cinnamon Cappuccino Ganache with Chocolate-
    Cinnamon Crunch, 108–109
-Cinnamon Crunch, 109
Cocoa Shells, *74*, 75
Cocoa Shells with Cacao Nibs, 75
Crunchy Cacao Nib Ganache, *106*, 107
Crunchy Hazelnut Gianduja Ganache, 126
Dark, Caramel, Creamy, *172*, 173
Earl Grey Ganache, 123
Fudgesicle, 179–180
Lapsang Souchong with Whiskey, 122–123
Lemon–Star Anise Ganache, *100*, 118–119
melting, 125
-Mint Ganache, *112*, 113–114
Peanut Gianduja Ganache, 127
Red Velvet Shells, 76
Sarah Bernhardts, 240, *241*
S'mores Filling, 216, *217*
-Tarragon Ganache, 114
tempering, 242
Cinnamon
    -Apple Butter with Calvados, 187
    Cappuccino Ganache with Chocolate-Cinnamon
        Crunch, 108–109
    -Chocolate Crunch, 109
    Shells, 84, *106*
Citrus, juicing and zesting, 77
Cocoa
    Red Velvet Shells, 76
    Shells, *74*, 75
    Shells with Cacao Nibs, 75
Coconut
    Caramel, 166–167
    German Chocolate Cake Filling, 206, *207*
    Shells, 68, *172*
Coffee. *See* Espresso
Compotes
    about, 185
    Ginger-Honey-Plum, 190, *194*
    Sour Cherry, 189

Confectioners' sugar, 17
Cream cheese
    Carrot Cake Filling, 209–210
    Red Velvet Cake Filling, 208
Cream of tartar, 20–21
Creamy fillings. *See also* Buttercreams
    Cherry-Almond Cream, 156
    curds, about, 129
    Ginger Cream, 69, 146–147
    Key Lime Curd, 150–151
    Lemon-Almond Cream, 157
    Lemon Curd, 149–150
    Orange Cream, 73, 145–146
    Passion Fruit Pastry Cream, 155
    pastry creams, about, 129
    Pear Cream, 148
    Popcorn Pastry Cream, 152, 153–154
    refrigerating, before using, 150
Crunch, Chocolate-Cinnamon, 109
Curds
    about, 129
    Key Lime, 150–151
    Lemon, 149–150
    refrigerating, before using, 150

D

Duck Confit with Port and Fig Filling, 234–235
Dulce de Leche Filling, 209

E

Earl Grey Ganache, 123
Egg whites
    "aged," note about, 19
    powdered, about, 20
    whipping, 26
    whisking, 18
Espresso
    Cinnamon Cappuccino Ganache with Chocolate-
    Cinnamon Crunch, 108–109
    Shells, 76, 161
Extracts, note about, 80

F

Fig and Port, Duck Confit with, 234–235
Fillings. *See also* American classics; Caramel fillings;
    Creamy fillings; Frozen fillings; Fruit-based fillings;
    Ganache; Savory fillings
    piping onto shells, 32–33, 63
Five Spice Shells, 85
Flavor compounds, about, 22–23, 80
Fleur de Sel Caramel, 160–162, *161*
Flour, nut-based. *See also* Almond flour
    making your own, 67
Foie Gras with Black Currant Gastrique Filling, 231–
    233, *232*
Food coloring, working with, 21–22, 66
French Macaron Method, Kathryn's Easiest, 55–58
French meringue, about, 34, 35
French Meringue Method, 40–44
Frozen fillings
    Almond Ice Milk, 176
    Anise Ice Milk, 177
    Chamomile Ice Milk, 182, *183*
    Fudgesicle, 179–180
    Honey Frozen Yogurt, 180
    notes about, 174, 175
    Orange-Buttermilk Ice Milk, 178
    Persimmon Ice Milk, 181
    scooping onto shells, 175
Fruit. *See also* Fruit-based fillings; *specific fruits*
    citrus, juicing and zesting, 77
    Fresh, Macaron Tarts, Open-Face, 243
Fruit-based fillings
    about, 185
    Apricot-Passion Pâte de Fruit, 199–200
    Apricot-Vanilla Jam, 191
    Blackberry Jelly, 198
    checking temperature of, 186
    Chile-Pineapple-Kumquat Marmalade, 192–193
    Cinnamon-Apple Butter with Calvados, 187
    Ginger-Honey-Plum Compote, 190, *194*
    Lemon Marmalade with Campari, *194*, 195–196

Pear Pâte de Fruit, 202
Pumpkin-Spice Butter, 188
Sour Cherry Compote, 189
spooning onto shells, 186
storing, 186
Strawberry-Guava Pâte de Fruit, 200–202, *201*
White Peach Jam, 197
Fruit butters
about, 185
Cinnamon-Apple Butter with Calvados, 187
Pumpkin-Spice Butter, 188
Fudgesicle, 179–180

G

Ganache
Cassis–White Chocolate, *93*, 124–125
Chai, 119–121, *120*
Chocolate-Mint, *112*, 113–114
Chocolate-Tarragon, 114
Cinnamon Cappuccino with Chocolate-Cinnamon
    Crunch, 108–109
cooling, tip for, 105
Crunchy Cacao Nib, *106*, 107
Crunchy Hazelnut Gianduja, 126
Earl Grey, 123
Green Tea and White Chocolate, 115
Lapsang Souchong with Whiskey, 122–123
Lemon–Star Anise, *100*, 118–119
Peanut Gianduja, 127
piping onto shells, 105
Rose-Raspberry, *90*, 110–111
White Chocolate-Grapefruit, 116–117
German Chocolate Cake Filling, *206*, 207
Ginger
-Apricot-Chocolate Caramel, 170–171
Cream, 69, 146–147
Gingerbread Buttercream, 144
-Honey-Plum Compote, 190, *194*
Shells, 85
Grapefruit–White Chocolate Ganache, 116–117
Green Tea and White Chocolate Ganache, 115

Green Tea Shells, 86, *87*
Guava-Strawberry Pâte de Fruit, 200–202, *201*

H

Hazelnut
Gianduja, Crunchy, Ganache, 126
Nougatine, 127
Shells, 68
Honey-Ginger-Plum Compote, 190, *194*
Honey Frozen Yogurt, 180
Hummus Filling, 220–221

I

Ice milk. *See under* Frozen fillings
Italian meringue, about, 34
Italian Meringue Method, 45–50

J

Jams
about, 185
Apricot-Vanilla, 191
White Peach, 197
Jelly, Blackberry, 198

K

Kathryn's Easiest French Macaron Method, 55–58
Key Lime Curd, 150–151
Key Lime with Marshmallow Fluff Filling, 212–214, *213*
Kumquat-Chile-Pineapple Marmalade, 192–193

L

Lapsang Souchong with Whiskey, 122–123
Lavender Shells, 89
Lemon(s)
-Almond Cream, 157
Curd, 149–150
juicing and zesting, 77
Marmalade with Campari, *194*, 195–196
-Poppyseed Shells, 78
Shells, 78
–Star Anise Ganache, *100*, 118–119

Licorice Shells, 79, *183*
Lime(s)
    juicing and zesting, 77
    Key, Curd, 150–151
    Key, with Marshmallow Fluff Filling, 212–214, *213*
    Shells, 78, *213*

M

Macadamia Shells, 68, 69
Macaronnage process, 26–27
Macarons
    alternate baking instructions, 256
    anatomy of, 14–15
    appearance and flavor, 13
    French-style versus American-style, 9
    history of, 10–12
    oven temperature issues, 256
    preparing, techniques for, 24–33
    primary ingredients, 16–18
    secondary ingredients, 20–23
    "skin and feet," 14–15
    troubleshooting guide, 249–255
Macarons, less-than-perfect
    Chocolate Beehives, *244*, 245–246
    Open-Face Fresh Fruit Macaron Tarts, 243
    Sarah Bernhardts, 240, *241*
    Trifle, 246–248, *247*
Macaron shells. *See also* Macaron shells (recipes)
    baked, cooling and removing, 31–32
    baked, filling, 32–33, 63
    baked, storing, 33
    baking, 31, 59–61
    baking times by size, 39
    base macaron methods, 34–39
    equipment for, 36
    folding ingredients together, 26–29
    macaronnage process, 26–27
    measuring ingredients for, 24
    piping onto baking sheet, 29–31, 59–61
    preparing baking sheets for, 25, 38
    savory, ingredient substitutions for, 95
    whipping egg whites for, 26

Macaron shells (recipes)
    Almond (French Meringue Method), 40–44
    Almond (Italian Meringue Method), 45–50
    Almond (Kathryn's Easiest French Macaron Method), 55–58
    Almond (Swiss Meringue Method), 51–54
    Ancho Chile, 102
    Blackberry, 81, *152*
    Black Pepper, *100*, 101
    Cardamom, 84
    Cashew, 68
    Cinnamon, 84, *106*
    Cocoa, *74*, 75
    Cocoa, with Cacao Nibs, 75
    Coconut, 68, *172*
    Espresso, 76, *161*
    Five Spice, 85
    Ginger, 85
    Green Tea, 86, *87*
    Hazelnut, 68
    Lavender, 89
    Lemon, 78
    Lemon-Poppyseed, 78
    Licorice, 79, *183*
    Lime, 78, *213*
    Macadamia, 68, 69
    Marigold, 88, *183*
    Mint, 80, *112*
    Orange, 77, *164*
    Parsley, 96, *97*
    Passion Fruit, 83, *120*
    Pecan, 68, 206
    Pink Peppercorn, 96, 101
    Pistachio, 70, *71*
    Red Velvet, 76
    Rose, 90, *91*
    Saffron, 98, *99*
    Sesame, 102, *227*
    Strawberry, 82, *201*
    Vanilla, 72, *73*
    Violet, 92, *93*
    Walnut, 68, 236

Wasabi, 103, *183*
Macaroons, American, description of, 9
Maple-Bacon-Bourbon Filling, *236*, 237
Maple Buttercream, 133
Marigold Shells, 88, *183*
Marmalades
    about, 185
    Chile-Pineapple-Kumquat, 192–193
    Lemon, with Campari, *194*, 195–196
Marshmallow Fluff with Key Lime Filling, 212–214, *213*
Meringue
    French, about, 34, 35
    French Method, 40–44
    Italian, about, 34
    Italian, Method, 45–50
    Swiss, about, 34
    Swiss, Method, 51–54
Mint-Chocolate Ganache, *112*, 113–114
Mint Shells, 80, *112*
Mushrooms and White Wine Filling, 223–224

N

Nougatine, Hazelnut, 127
Nut(s). *See also specific types of nuts*
    flour, making your own, 67
    toasting, 135

O

Oatmeal Cookie Buttercream, 141–142
Orange(s)
    Blood, Caramel, *164*, 165–166
    -Buttermilk Ice Milk, 178
    Cream, *73*, 145–146
    juicing and zesting, 77
    Shells, 77, *164*

P

Parchment paper, 25
Parsley Shells, 96, 97
Passion Fruit
    Apricot-Passion Pâte de Fruit, 199–200
    Pastry Cream, 155

Shells, 83, *120*
Pastry Creams
    about, 129
    Passion Fruit, 155
    Popcorn, *152*, 153–154
Pâte de Fruits
    about, 185
    Apricot-Passion, 199–200
    Pear, 202
    Strawberry-Guava, 200–202, *201*
Peach, White, Jam, 197
Peanut butter
    Peanut Gianduja Ganache, 127
    Thai Chile–Peanut Filling, 225–226
Pear Cream, 148
Pear Pâte de Fruit, 202
Pecan(s)
    German Chocolate Cake Filling, *206*, 207
    Shells, 68, *206*
Pectin, yellow, about, 203
Persimmon Ice Milk, 181
Piña Colada Filling, Tropical, 214–215
Pineapple
    -Chile-Kumquat Marmalade, 192–193
    Tropical Piña Colada Filling, 214–215
Pink Peppercorn Shells, 96, 101
Pistachio(s)
    Buttercream, 134–135
    Shells, *70*, 71
    toasting, 135
Plum-Ginger-Honey Compote, 190, *194*
Popcorn Pastry Cream, *152*, 153–154
Poppyseed-Lemon Shells, 78
Port and Fig, Duck Confit with, 234–235
Powdered egg whites, about, 20
Praline paste
    Crunchy Hazelnut Gianduja Ganache, 126
Pumpkin
    Gingerbread Buttercream, 144
    -Spice Butter, 188

R

Raisins
    Carrot Cake Filling, 209–210
    Oatmeal Cookie Buttercream, 141–142
Raspberry-Rose Ganache, 90, 110–111
Raspberry–White Chocolate Caramel, 168–169
Red Velvet
    Cake Filling, 208
    Shells, 76
Resources, 257–260
Rosemary Caramel, 162–163
Rosemary-Chèvre Filling, 96, 222–223
Rose-Raspberry Ganache, 90, 110–111
Rose Shells, 90, 91

S

Saffron Shells, 98, 99
Salt, 21
Sarah Bernhardts, 240, 241
Savory fillings
    about, 219
    Chèvre-Rosemary, 96, 222–223
    Chicken Mole, 229–230
    Duck Confit with Port and Fig, 234–235
    Foie Gras with Black Currant Gastrique, 231–233, 232
    Hummus, 220–221
    Maple-Bacon-Bourbon, 236, 237
    Mushrooms and White Wine, 223–224
    spooning onto shells, 219
    Thai Chile-Peanut, 225–226
    Tomato Confit, 226–228, 227
Sesame seeds
    Sesame Brittle, 140
    Sesame Buttercream, 139–140
    Sesame Shells, 102, 227
Silicone mats, 25
S'mores Filling, 216, 217
Sour Cherry Compote, 189
Star Anise-Lemon Ganache, 100, 118–119

Strawberry Guava Pâte de Fruit, 200–202, 201
Strawberry Shells, 82, 201
Sugar, confectioners', 17
Sugar, granulated, 18
Sugar syrup, testing temperature of, 130
Swiss meringue, about, 34
Swiss Meringue Method, 51–54

T

Tarragon-Chocolate Ganache, 114
Tarts, Open-Face Fresh Fruit Macaron, 243
Tea
    Earl Grey Ganache, 123
    Green Tea and White Chocolate Ganache, 116–117
    Green Tea Shells, 86, 87
    Lapsang Souchong with Whiskey, 122–123
Thai Chile-Peanut Filling, 225–226
Tomato Confit Filling, 226–228, 227
Trifle, 246–248, 247
Tropical Piña Colada Filling, 214–215

V

Vanilla Buttercream, 87, 131–132
Vanilla Shells, 72, 73
Violet Shells, 92, 93

W

Walnut Shells, 68, 236
Wasabi Shells, 103, 183
Whiskey, Lapsang Souchong with, 122–123
White Chocolate
    –Cassis Ganache, 93, 124–125
    –Grapefruit Ganache, 116–117
    and Green Tea Ganache, 115
    –Raspberry Caramel, 168–169
    Rose-Raspberry Ganache, 90, 110–111
White Peach Jam, 197

Y

Yellow pectin, about, 203
Yogurt, Honey Frozen, 180